M·O·S·A·I·C™ QUICK TOUR

FOR WINDOWS

Accessing and Navigating the Internet's World Wide Web

Gareth Branwyn

VENTANA PRESS

Mosaic Quick Tour for Windows: Accessing & Navigating the Internet's World Wide Web

ISBN: 1-56604-194-5

Book design: Marcia Webb
Cover design: Spring Davis-Charles, One-of-a-Kind Design; Dawne Sherman
Cover illustration: David Watts
Index service: Mark Kmetzko
Technical advisor: Sean Carton
Technical review: Gary Moore
Editorial staff: Angela Anderson, Walter R. Bruce, III, Diana Merelman, Pam Richardson, Jessica Ryan
Production staff: Patrick Berry, Dan Koeller, Dawne Sherman, Marcia Webb
Proofreader: Eric Edstam

First Edition 9 8 7 6 5 4 3 2
Printed in the United States of America

Ventana Press, Inc.
P.O. Box 2468
Chapel Hill, NC 27515
919/942-0220
FAX 919/942-1140

TRADEMARKS

Trademarked names appear throughout this book. Rather than list the names and entities that own the trademarks or insert a trademark symbol with each mention of the trademarked name, the publisher states that it is using the names only for editorial purposes and to the benefit of the trademark owner with no intention of infringing upon that trademark.

ABOUT THE AUTHOR

Gareth Branwyn is a freelance writer and hypermedia designer. He is a regular contributor to *Wired* magazine, the senior editor of *bOING bOING* (a pop culture humor mag) and the former Street Tech editor of *Mondo 2000*. His book publishing credits include chapters in *Mondo 2000's User's Guide to the New Edge* (HarperPerennial, 1992), *Flame Wars* (Duke University Press, 1994), *Virtual Reality Casebook* (Van Nostrand Reinhold, 1994), *The Multimedia Home Companion* (Warner Books, 1995) and *The Millennial Whole Earth Catalog* (Harper San Francisco, 1994). He is currently co-editing *bOING bOING's Happy Mutant Handbook* (Putnam Berkeley, 1995). As a hypermedia designer he is co-creator of the critically acclaimed *Beyond Cyberpunk!*, an electronic compendium of cyberculture. Gareth has been a flag-waving Net citizen since 1987.

ACKNOWLEDGMENTS

First and foremost I want to thank Sean Carton. He was my right-hand man on this project and contributed ideas, material, Net wisdom and ace datasurfing talents, all beyond the call of duty. This is his book too.

The other members of my book team were my wife Pam and son Blake. They helped to keep my spirits up, shoved food under my office door and kept me from yakking on the phone when I was supposed to be working. Alberto Gaitan also gets a pat on the back for his technical assistance and suggestions.

I'd also like to thank the software developers at NCSA for making such a great piece of freeware. The authors of all the freeware and shareware covered in this book are to be thanked and commended. It was a great feeling to be working on a book where lots of the software covered is available free to anyone who has the means to download it. And it's not just free software, it's *good* free software.

CONTENTS

5

INTRODUCTION

Imagine the world's largest living document—thousands and thousands of text, graphic, audio and video files interlinked throughout the world. Well that's the World Wide Web, and Mosaic is your key to that world.

The guide you hold in your hands is your entry into the world of hypermedia. Inside you'll learn Mosaic's simple graphic interface, the functions of its many menus and user-configurable features, and most importantly, how to use its navigation tools so you can effortlessly scramble through the hypermedia web that's been cast over the Internet. With Mosaic, you'll be able to view online magazines, complete with graphics, sounds and even moving images. You'll be able to ask "robot librarians" to help you search the Net for information. These automated programs will worm their way through the Net and report their findings back to you. Whether it's recreation, education, art and literature, or the latest in computer technology you're looking for, you can easily find it on the Net with Mosaic as your guide. In fact, Mosaic is not only a hypermedia information browser, you can also use it to access many standard Internet services such as Gopher, WAIS, FTP and USENET News (read only). All this makes Mosaic, and its forthcoming commercial offspring, the platform to watch as the Internet continues to make its way into the mainstream of American life.

The "catch" here is that to use Mosaic, you'll need a full-blown Internet connection. If you're not sure whether you can justify an Internet hook-up or you're unsure of what type you need, read on...

Decisions, Decisions...

All Net connections are not created equal. They can run from cheap email-only accounts to expensive direct lines. Today, the question is not "Do I need to connect?" as much as "*How* do I connect?" Choosing a method of Net access doesn't have to mean a descent into the pit of computer geekdom, weird acronyms and impenetrable jargon. However, you *will* need to decide on a few things beforehand:

- Do I need a direct, SLIP/PPP or standard dial-up connection?
- How fast a connection do I need?
- How much do I want to spend?

Internet connections are usually divided into three types:

- Direct, or "dedicated," connections (between your computer and the Internet).

  Dedicated connections are the most desirable because they give you access to all the Internet services (including things like Mosaic and Internet radio), at high speeds, 24 hours a day.

- Temporary dial-up, commonly called "SLIP/PPP," connections (your connection is routed through a local service provider).

  This is a less expensive alternative to the direct connection. Using a standard high-speed modem (14,400 baud) and special software, you can fool your home computer into thinking it's a big wheel on the information superhighway.

- Dial-up accounts (your computer becomes a terminal on a local host computer that's connected to the Internet).

  On a dial-up account, you phone into a Net-connected computer where you have an "account." With this type of indirect or "host" connection, all of your interactions with the Internet are through programs that run on the host machine. When you read email and USENET News, transfer files or do anything else, you can only use programs (usually text-based, icky UNIX programs) that run on the host. This type of connection is cheap and perfectly adequate if all you're looking for are the basic services like email, telnet, FTP, Gopher and newsgroups. Unfortunately, you cannot run Mosaic, HGopher, Eudora or any of the other programs mentioned in this book with this type of account.

Note: You may even be directly connected to the Net already! If you use a locally networked computer at a large institution or corporation, you may already be wired into the Net and not even know it. Check with your systems administrator.

Super-Duper Mosaic Quick Start

Luckily, Mosaic is fairly easy to learn and simple to use. Once you have your SLIP/PPP (or other network) connection running, all you do is double-click on the Mosaic icon and you will be automatically logged into the Home Page at the National Center for Supercomputing Applications (NCSA). Welcome to Mosaic! From the Home Page, you can read the introductory information, click on *hyperlinks* (highlighted in blue) and browse through online demos and documentation (located under the "Help" menu). When you're through being a big shot and wandering around on your own, you can either (1) proceed to the "Mosaic Quick Peek" section in Chapter 2, or (2) browse the following chapter synopses to find out where to go next.

What's Inside

Chapter 1, "The Net & the Web," provides a brief look at the Internet's recent growth rate and the wild and wacky metaphors that are often used to describe this exciting and ever-changing electronic world. Also covered are the circuitous history of hypermedia, the surprising emergence of the World Wide Web, a hypermedia system for the Internet, and the growing popularity of Mosaic, the free "front-end" software that lets you explore the Web.

Chapter 2, "Getting Started," gives instructions on how to get Mosaic up and running on your machine. It covers what hardware and software you need, where to find Mosaic on the Internet and how to download it, unzip it and configure it for use. Read the "Mosaic Quick Peek" section to learn more about Mosaic's main navigation features.

Chapter 3, "Cruising Mosaic's Menus," provides a detailed tour of all the features offered in Mosaic. Includes menu items, navigating and using URLs, hyperlinks, inline images and hyperlinked media, installing Helper Applications and changing type styles.

Chapter 4, "Web Walking With Mosaic," covers how to use Mosaic to keep up with what's happening in cyberspace by taking you on a jaunt through the Web and by discussing how to use Mosaic for accessing Internet services such as FTP, telnet, newsgroup reading and Gopher; how to create your own Web documents; how to get and use additional TCP/IP applications; and how to link up with others using and discussing Mosaic.

Chapter 5, "Site Seeing," lists a directory of Web documents useful for beginners as well as sites offering libraries, look-up services and a diverse range of cool hypermedia resources available to Mosaic users.

Appendix A details the new features found in Mosaic 2.x. Appendix B covers many of the common error messages found in Mosaic 2.x.

A complete glossary, bibliography and index are also included.

Hardware & Software Requirements

Before we begin there are some basic hardware and software requirements that must be met to access the Internet through Mosaic.

To run Windows Mosaic with all of its Helper Applications, you need to be able to run Windows 3.1 in 386 Enhanced mode with the Win32s upgrade (for 32-bit addressing). The reason for Enhanced mode is so that Windows can use virtual memory.

- A 386 SX w/4mb RAM (absolute minimum).
- A 486/33 w/8mb RAM is strongly recommended.
- If you want to view images and movies, you will need an SVGA monitor.
- Microsoft Windows 3.1 in 386 Enhanced mode.
- Microsoft's Win32s software upgrade (current version 1.1.5a).
- A 1.1-compliant winsock.dll.
- A 14,400 baud modem (or faster).
- A SLIP or PPP dial-up Internet account (or a direct connection).
- A TCP/IP protocol stack (SLIP/PPP communications software).

Helper Application Requirements

Mosaic uses a suite of other programs to handle the presentation of graphics, movies and sound. If you want to make use of these resources (and you will!), you'll need a true color SVGA card and a sound card (such as SoundBlaster). If you want to use the QuickTime movie player, you will need the current version of QuickTime for Windows. See Chapter 3 for complete details on obtaining and configuring Helper Applications.

How to Use *Mosaic Quick Tour*

This book was written using the Alpha 6 version of Mosaic 2.x. By the time you read this, there will probably be higher Alpha versions, or maybe even the full-blown 2.0 release. Regardless of what version of Mosaic you're using, from 1.x to 2.x, the documentation in *Mosaic Quick Tour* will be applicable. In 2.x, some of the features have been expanded and a few things have been added, such as forms support. The menus have also gone through some rearrangement, but most of the features and functions they offer remain unchanged. As I write this, a number of commercial versions of Mosaic are also under development. Hopefully they will stay close enough to the current freeware versions so that what you learn in this *Quick Tour* will be directly relevant or easily translatable.

Mosaic and the World Wide Web it accesses are experiencing a period of intense growth—changes occur daily. This book and its *Online Companion* are designed to provide you with the basic knowledge and resources you need to navigate your own course through this newest wrinkle in cyberspace. Once you've made it into the main current of the data flow, you should have no trouble keeping up with the changes as they happen. It's an exciting time to be on the Net.

Ventana Visitors Center To stay abreast of all late-breaking news and information on Mosaic, the World Wide Web and *Mosaic Quick Tour*, why not add the Ventana Visitors Center to your hotlists menu, or better yet, make it your home page! The Visitors Center's URL is **http://www.vmedia.com/vvc** (see Chapter 3 for details). At the Center you can also get the latest versions of Mosaic, the default Helper Applications and many of the other excellent freeware and shareware programs mentioned in this book. If you have no idea what I'm talking about, don't worry—that's why I wrote this book.

And, welcome to Mosaic, the future face of the Net that you can use today!

HOT TIP

When I teach computer classes, I always tell my students, "Don't be intimidated by the size of the manual and the sense that you have to memorize everything." The trick to gaining an upper hand with new software is knowing what things are called and how to look them up. If the book has a good index, and you know the terms, you can find the information you need, when you need it. *Mosaic Quick Tour* has a glossary of most of the keywords you'll encounter in Mosaic. Familiarize yourself with them, and looking things up will be much easier.

So, dear friend, grab a cup of coffee (catnip tea, or whatever you drink), park yourself in your hydraulic ergonomic chair, fire up the ol' PC and get ready to jack into hyperspace.

Into the future,
Gareth Branwyn
July 1994
gareth@vmedia.com

THE NET & THE WEB

I got a message from a friend the other day. He said his Mom was now on the Internet and had sent him a message saying, "Why don't you ever send me any email?"
- Heard on the Net

Everyone is pouring into cyberspace. Just a few years ago, friends' and family members' eyes would glaze over whenever I would start talking about the Internet. They'd get that "Uh oh, he's talking about geek stuff" look on their faces and they'd start nodding politely (or nodding off) till I was through with my little Net sermon. Now, many of these same people have Internet addresses printed on their business cards!

The Net has become hip, essential to modern life. Ma, Pa and the kids want in on the action. Trolling the Net looking for news stories has become a full-time job for journalists and TV talk-show researchers. The business community is also hitching up its wagon trains and heading into the vast uncharted territory of cyberspace.

Current estimates put the size of the Internet at over 2 million sites and over 20 million users worldwide. While these figures are hotly debated by Net statisticians, and increasing as I write this, they give you some idea of the magnitude of this mushrooming electronic world.

Given the invisible, almost mystical nature of cyberspace, grasping for metaphors is a common pastime among Net enthusiasts. "Superhighway" and "lawless frontier" are the most frequent allusions. "Mushrooms" may be as apt as anything else. On a daily basis, networks and sites, large and small, pop up, like fungal growth in the fertile loam of ever-cheapening hardware, software and network access. This, coupled with the evangelism and hard work of thousands of Net pioneers, has led to phenomenal growth. The Internet and its constituent networks have created a global "cooperative anarchy," neither centrally located nor centrally administrated. It is growing "organically," without the benefit (or burden) of a master plan.

Another apt analogy for the Net can be drawn from Neil Stephenson's recent cyberpunk novel *Snow Crash* (1992). In Stephenson's near-future world, a floating city is being formed off the coast of California. Attracted by a mysterious cult figure, thousands of people, in ships, yachts, motor boats and anything else that floats, are attaching themselves to this huge flotilla. Decks, gangways, planked walkways and bridges connect the ever-growing mass. The Internet is much like this structure (minus the evil cult leader). People have become so attracted to the services, information mother lode and virtual community offered by the Net that they're using whatever means they can to float into it. Some come in tiny boats (SLIP/PPP connections), others on huge cruisers and fancy yachts (workstations, government and university systems). But once connected, all have at their disposal access to the electronic city, floating in the mysterious ethers of cyberspace.

While all these metaphors are limiting, and ultimately silly, they are a fun way of visualizing this new realm of technoculture, and they sometimes come in handy when explaining the life and structure of the Internet to newcomers. The reigning metaphors that frame this book and the world it explores are webs—webs as elegant, interlaced pieces of fabric, and webs as spider's lairs that ensnare all that wander into them.

As the Internet (the Net for short) has spread across the globe, users have struggled to find better ways of making more efficent use of its expanding resources. The World Wide Web, a system for linking, or weaving together, the far-flung resources of the Internet is one recent answer to this problem. But this system simply makes data sites on the Net capable of being woven together. Something is needed to combine the disparate parts into a whole. That something is Mosaic, a program that brings a new level of information access, bandwidth and organization to the Internet. But we're getting a little ahead of ourselves. Let's take a look at some of the historical precedents that led to the emergence of the Web.

The Curious Growth of Hypermedia

When Apple Computer released HyperCard for the Macintosh in 1987, no one really knew what to make of it, or exactly how to use it. It was the first widely available program to create hypertext, an idea that had been floating around the computer industry and academia since Ted Nelson began promoting it in 1965.

Hypertext is a means of linking computer-based documents in associative, nonlinear ways. For example, this is how hypertext could work: You're reading a biography of Abraham Lincoln and you come to a reference to the Gettysburg Address. Simply by clicking on the words "Gettysburg Address," you can be linked to the full text of that famous speech. After reading it, you can either go back to your place in the Lincoln bio, or you can click on other links within the Gettysburg Address, wandering down an information pathway that you make up as you go along.

Early promoters of hypertext hailed it as a revolution in learning, allowing one to combine linear study with self-exploration and chance discovery. Oddly enough, HyperCard, created by Apple programming visionary Bill Atkinson, was not actually intended as a hypertext program, although that turned out to be one of its most intriguing features. Bundled free with all new Macs, HyperCard was easy to use and yet quite sophisticated. It not only had hypertext capabilities, but also offered the ability to manage and link everything from paint images to audio samples and external media devices like video disc players. Subsequent releases of HyperCard, and the other programs that followed, added the ability to link up additional graphic formats, animations and even desktop movies. This combination of hypertext and multimedia was dubbed "hypermedia." Surprisingly, people continued to struggle with the concept of hypermedia and how it could best be used. Even today, while the field of multimedia has grown, especially with the recent explosion of CD-ROM, many of the available multimedia titles make scant use of the hypertext concept. People *still* don't seem to understand what hypertext and hypermedia are all about.

It took a group of physicists from Geneva, Switzerland, to give hypermedia the big developmental boost it needed.

Is Mosaic Like Xanadu? When introduced to Mosaic, many people ask if it is the realization of Ted Nelson's vision of Xanadu, a hypothetical worldwide hypertext system encompassing *all* written information. The answer is yes...and no. While Mosaic (and the WWW it accesses) is a hypertext/hypermedia system that spans the globe, interlinking terabytes of information, there are differences between Mosaic and Xanadu.

- Mosaic is available free of charge, and access to many of the resources it connects to is free of charge. Xanadu is intended to be a "pay-per-view" system in which each data search is charged to you and your search results can be sold to others.
- Xanadu is not intended to be a front end for the Internet; it has one basic function. Mosaic is more than just a hypertext system; it can access most Internet services.
- Mosaic actually exists. After decades of development and hype, Xanadu is still a fantasy. →

The Weaving of the Web

Created at the European Particle Physics Laboratory (CERN) in Geneva, the World Wide Web (abbreviated "WWW") was originally conceived of as a Net-based hypertext exchange system that would allow European physicists to share a "universe of documents." As soon as the first implementation of the Web concept was introduced in 1991, enthusiasm quickly grew beyond the bounds of CERN and the scientific community. Computer programmers from around the world, excited by the possibilities of "hyperlinking" documents throughout the Internet, began developing Web applications and promoting the World Wide Web online. Early users also realized that not only hypertext, but full-blown hypermedia, could be passed over the Internet using Web technology.

It now looks as though hypermedia is finally going to make an impact, but in a way that its pioneers never would have expected.

- Xanadu would be a stand-alone system. Mosaic takes advantage of the already-existing infrastructure of the Internet.
- Xanadu would be centrally administrated by a commercial entity. Mosaic is essentially decentralized and free of any one entity's control.

For more information on Xanadu, check out: http://www.aus.xanadu.com/

Mosaic: Free & Easy

Soon after the introduction of the World Wide Web, software designers at the National Center for Supercomputing Applications (NCSA) at the University of Illinois, Urbana-Champaign, began work on a simple and powerful graphical interface for WWW. With many similarities to HyperCard, Mosaic was designed to be an easy-to-use, easy-to-build hypermedia system operated via pop-up windows, pull-down menus and "point-and-click" navigation. Except here, rather than weaving your way through the media available on a single disk drive, you weave your way through the vast resources of the Internet! Mosaic's first release in June 1993 (for X Windows) was met with great enthusiasm. Versions for Windows and Mac soon followed. Perhaps more than any other piece of WWW software, Mosaic has helped fuel an explosion of interest in the World Wide Web and the possibilities of building a true "hypermedia universe" in cyberspace.

Why Is NCSA's Mosaic So Great?

It's free! NCSA is a federally funded institution, one of four National Science Foundation supercomputing centers. One of NCSA's missions is to provide noncommercial software that can benefit the scientific community. In accomplishing this goal, NCSA has made Mosaic readily available on the Internet, to the benefit of all. In addition to its free status, Mosaic

- Runs over a SLIP/PPP connection.
- Is easy to install and intuitive to use.
- Features a simple interface using common windows/menu format and mouse-driven navigation.
- Offers online help and email technical support.
- Allows you to change type styles, size and format (bold, italic) on the documents you're browsing.
- Supports audio, movies (MPEG and QuickTime) and graphics (GIF, JPEG).
- Offers a "History" feature that lets you retrace your steps.
- Provides access to network services such as USENET News (read only), FTP and Gopher.
- Allows you to create and store lists of frequently used documents.
- Includes a personal "Annotations" feature that lets you add written notes to any Mosaic document (for your eyes only). You can also share these annotations with a workgroup.
- Includes a "Search" feature that allows you to search through indexes within documents.

- Is a client/server program, meaning your connection time is limited to only as long as it takes Mosaic (the client) to send your request for information. A connection is reopened when the host computer (the server) is ready to respond to your request. This scheme cuts down on Net traffic.
- Fully supports HTTP (HyperText Transport Protocol) and HTML (HyperText Markup Language), the current standards for WWW communication and presentation of information.

What in Cyberspace Is HTML?

HTML, or HyperText Markup Language, is the language the World Wide Web speaks. Web documents written in HTML contain formatting codes that tell Web browsing software (such as Mosaic) how to present the various components of a document to the user. HTML is so simple to use that many Web users have become Web producers. Similar to the rapid proliferation and exchange of HyperCard stacks generated soon after that program's release, HTML has fostered a boon in creating WWW documents. The beauty of webbed hypermedia is that, once Web-accessible, it can be hyperlinked to other sites, building, organically, that vast universe of hypermedia now under construction.

What Does the Future Hold?

Without sounding too grandiose, it is possible that Mosaic and its progeny could quickly become the standard front end for the Internet. Even though Internet "membership" is growing rapidly, many users have great difficulty figuring out how to use all the available services. This, coupled with the infoglut of too much information and no way of burrowing through it, means that the Internet experience can quickly become overwhelming. Mosaic brings the resources of the Internet back into the familiar realm of the Windows and Mac graphic user environments. Few average users know what an IP address is, or how to write a UNIX script; but almost everyone knows how to point and click a mouse.

For many Internet service developers, Mosaic is a major breakthrough. Government agencies, universities, mail-order businesses and publishers (to name a few) are all scrambling to offer their resources through Mosaic. Mitch Kapor, founder of the Electronic Frontier Foundation (EFF) and a chief evangelist for the information highway, sees Mosaic as a major turning point in providing free and open access.

Another likely area of development for Mosaic may be as a full-blown Internet publisher. Numerous magazines have been exploring better ways of making the leap into cyberspace, and Mosaic might be the ticket. As the software improves and modem speeds increase, full-page layouts with color graphics, animations, film clips, automated product ordering and many other features will become commonplace. Using Mosaic for video-on-demand and set-top-box interactive television is also a likely possibilility.

Given the "cooperative anarchy" under which Mosaic has thus far been built and distributed, we should also expect the unexpected when thinking about its future.

Let Me Get This Straight

If you're having trouble figuring all this out, let's recap.

The Internet The global "network of networks" is currently comprised of over 2 million computer sites and over 20 million users. The Net is the physical hardware of computers, gateways, bridges, telephone connections and the software that runs everything.

The World Wide Web The World Wide Web is a hypermedia exchange system that allows users to exchange linked text, images and sounds over the Internet. Abbreviated as WWW.

Hypertext & Hypermedia Hypertext is a means of linking information in a document to allow the reader to explore non-linear connections to other documents (or parts of the same document). Hypermedia is the same concept, expanded to include graphics, moving images and sounds.

HTML HyperText Markup Language (or HTML) is simply the language that all World Wide Web documents "speak."

Mosaic A program that allows you to explore the resources available via the World Wide Web is called a *browser*. Mosaic is a popular WWW browser that uses a mouse-driven graphic interface to make Web navigating easy.

Moving On

The Internet is big. We've all been witness to its amazing growth and its overshadowing hype in the media. Hype abounds—and now that hype has been turned toward the World Wide Web and Mosaic. Is this latest development as cool as people say it is? Let's look beyond the hype to some of the numbers. According to *Entering the World Wide Web*, an electronic document created by Kevin Hughes, Web growth has been phenomenal. He reports that a software "robot" was sent through the Web in June of 1993 to count all the sites offering WWW documents. This robot logged around 100 sites. In May of 1994, a similar automated traveler wove its way through 3,800 Web sites. Hughes goes on to report that the folks at NCSA, makers of Mosaic and maintainers of one of the busiest Web sites in the world, claim that they get at least 1 million connections to their site *per week*—and the number is increasing swiftly. Just one year ago, that number was 100,000 connections per week. Given this level of activity, it's clear that Mosaic and WWW *are* all the rage in cyberspace. This book gives you the information and skills you need to access the Web yourself so you can see what all the fuss is about.

So, your interest has been piqued and you're caught up on some Net and Web history; now it's time to get busy. The following chapter covers all the basics on how to find Mosaic on the Net, how to set it up on your computer and how to take your first trip through the Web. My job will be to make all this sound easy. Wish us both luck.

2

GETTING STARTED

A journey of a thousand miles begins with a full tank of gas.
– *Anonymous*

Our trip is going to be a short one, so let's get down to business. This tour guide is not for Net novices. I'm assuming you're already familiar with Microsoft Windows, modems, basic telecommunications and the Internet. If you are unfamiliar with the Internet, I recommend you read Michael Fraase's *Windows Internet Tour Guide* (Ventana Press), or some other introductory book. (See the bibliography for more suggestions.) If you already have some form of File Transfer Protocol (FTP) access (such as a dial-up account), you can download electronic versions of Brendan P. Kehoe's *Zen and the Art of the Internet* from ftp.cs.widener.edu or *The Hitchhiker's Guide to the Internet* from ftp.eff.org. Search the EFF site for numerous other Net-related documents.

In this chapter you'll be given the information you need to find and download Mosaic using conventional FTP on a dial-up account. You can also download it using Windows-based programs such as Chameleon FTP and Winsock FTP over a SLIP/PPP connection (details to follow). After you've wrangled Mosaic onto your hard drive and unpacked it, I'll show you how to do a basic configuration of it so you can jump into the Web immediately to have a quick look around.

Necessary Connections

If you are already on the Net and have Mosaic downloaded but still need to install it, skip this section and move on to "Unpacking Your Booty" on page 20. To run Mosaic, you need either a direct (or "dedicated") Internet connection (found in many businesses, government offices and universities), or you need what's called a SLIP (Serial Line Internet Protocol) or PPP (Point-to-Point Protocol) account. Many local Internet service providers now offer SLIP/PPP connections at very reasonable rates. In some cases, the cost of the SLIP/PPP connection is not a lot more than a standard dial-up account. As these types of connections become more common, thanks in part to the growing popularity of Mosaic, service providers are making SLIP/PPP connections easier to get and to set up. Call your local provider for more information.

HOT TIP

For an updated electronic list of Internet service providers, Peter Kaminski's PDIAL list is highly recommended. To get a current copy of the list, send an email message to info-deli-server@netcom.com with the message **Send PDIAL**. If you do not yet have Net access, and therefore cannot get this list, have a wired friend download it for you.

There are two other pieces of software you'll need to acquire and install before you can get Mosaic up and running. Let's take a look at them.

The TCP/IP Protocol Stack

To make use of your SLIP/PPP connection, once you have it, you'll need to install a TCP/IP protocol stack. This is a program that handles the data transmissions between your PC and the rest of the Internet. If you're using the Chameleon Sampler disk that came with *The Windows Internet Tour Guide* or the *Internet Membership Kit*, you already have all the connection software you need (its TCP/IP stack is called NEWT). If you don't already have TCP/IP connection software, there are several freeware/shareware packages you can download. I recommend the shareware program Trumpet Winsock. You can download it via FTP from NCSA's FTP server located at ftp.ncsa.uiuc.edu in the directory /PC/Mosaic/sockets, or from ftp.utas.edu.au in the directory /pc/trumpet/winsock. Make sure you download both winsock.zip (the TCP/IP protocol stack) and winapps.zip (the Trumpet Winsock applications). See below for information on FTPing and unpacking transferred files.

Note: If you're using a TCP/IP stack other than NEWT or Trumpet Winsock, you may need to install a small program called a driver *before you can connect with the Net. Consult the documentation that comes with the TCP/IP stack to find out if you'll need such a driver. Also, don't be afraid to consult with your Internet service provider or your network administrator.*

Win32s for Windows

Once you have your TCP/IP software configured (get the necessary configuration information from your Internet service provider), you'll need to install a special upgrade for Microsoft Windows 3.1 to be able to run Mosaic 2.x. (If you're running under Windows NT, you are already in 32-bit mode and won't need Win32s. Fr*om now on I'll assume you're running Windows 3.1.*) From version 2.0A3 on, Mosaic has been a 32-bit application. The Win32s upgrade is available by FTP from ftp.ncsa.uiuc.edu in the /PC/Mosaic directory or directly from Microsoft at ftp.microsoft.com. The current version is called win32s115.zip. The file will be transferred in the .zip data compression format. See below for information on FTPing and unpacking transferred files.

Note: If you are running a 32-bit application, you already have Win32s installed in your system. Check to see if you have a subdirectory called Win32s under your Windows\System subdirectory. If you do, you will not have to download and install it again.

Important Note: Win32s is not compatible with OS/2. If you have an OS/2 system, you'll need to use Mosaic 2 Alpha 2, the last version of the program that's 16-bit. Since Alpha 3, Mosaic has been 32-bit.

HOT TIP

It is a commonly held belief that SLIP/PPP connections are expensive, and that the software is difficult to configure. This may have *been* the case, but the recent increased interest among Internet users for this type of connection has led to the widespread availability of free or inexpensive TCP/IP software. Several popular book/software packages such as *The Windows Internet Tour Guide* (Ventana Press) and the *Internet Membership Kit* (Ventana Media) provide all the software you need. Many Internet service providers have developed helpful scripts and installation instructions, and will walk you through the connection procedure over the phone if necessary. Several providers will even configure the software for you. Call around and find a provider that can give you the level of assistance you need. Don't be scared away from this type of connectivity. It's easier than you think.

Downloading Mosaic

Once you have your Internet connection taken care of, and Win32s installed, you're ready to download and install Mosaic.

Note: Obviously you don't have to download and install the TCP/IP software, Win32s and Mosaic separately. Since they are all available from the NCSA site, you can download them all at the same time using the following procedure.

Using Traditional FTP on a Dial-up Account

If you have a regular dial-up Internet account, you can get all the files you need for Mosaic by anonymous FTP. Here's how:

1. Create a subdirectory on your hard drive called Mosaic (or whatever you care to call it).

2. With your communications program, log onto your user account as you normally would.

3. At the prompt, type **ftp ftp.ncsa.uiuc.edu**

(The double ftp is not a mistake: the first ftp is the command; the second is part of the address of the FTP site.)

4. Press Enter and you will soon be connected to the NCSA FTP server.

5. At the login prompt, type **anonymous**. When asked for a password, type in your full Internet email address (username@site.domain). This is a common network convention used with FTP logins, hence the frequently used term "anonymous FTP."

Note: If you have trouble connecting to the NCSA site, see the list of other FTP "mirror" sites in Table 2-1.

6. Once inside the FTP server, you'll want to change to the directory that contains the Mosaic files. That command is cd PC/Mosaic.

Note: Unlike DOS's backslash, the Net uses UNIX's forward slash as the subdirectory delimiter.

7. From inside the Mosaic file area, type **ls** and press Enter. That's the UNIX command for a directory list. Among the items listed, you should see wmos20a6r1.zip (or whatever the latest version is called).

8. The .zip extension on the end of the file name indicates that the file has been compressed with PKWare's ZIP utility and stored as a binary file. You'll need to tell the host computer you want it downloaded as a binary file by typing **bin**. It should respond with "Type set to I" (the "I" stands for image file, or binary).

9. To retrieve the program, type **get wmos20a6r1.zip** (or whatever the file is currently called). The file will then be transferred.

10. If you haven't already downloaded Win32s (and Trumpet Winsock, if needed), you can do so at this time. Win32s is located in the same directory under the name win32s11.zip. Trumpet Winsock is located in the next subdirectory in /PC/Mosaic/sockets.

> *Note: If you're on a dial-up connection, the file will be downloaded to your local host computer. Consult the manual provided with your dial-up Internet account (and your modem software manual) if you are unfamiliar with how to get the file from their machine to yours.*

Using a Windows-based FTP Program

If you have TCP/IP FTP software up and running (such as Chameleon FTP or WS-FTP), you can use it to easily download the programs you need. See the instructions that came with the software on how to configure it for FTPing. When you're ready to log on,

1. Create a subdirectory on your hard drive called Mosaic (or whatever you care to call it).

2. Launch the FTP program and set the program for Binary file transfer. See Figure 2-1.

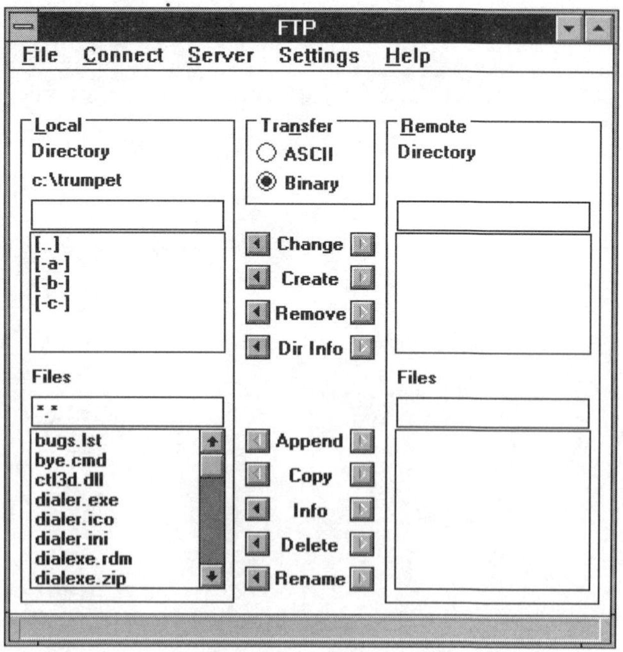

Figure 2-1: *A typical FTP transfer window.*

3. Type **ftp.ncsa.uiuc.edu** in the appropriate box. (In Chameleon FTP, this is entered under the Connect menu item.) See Figure 2-2.

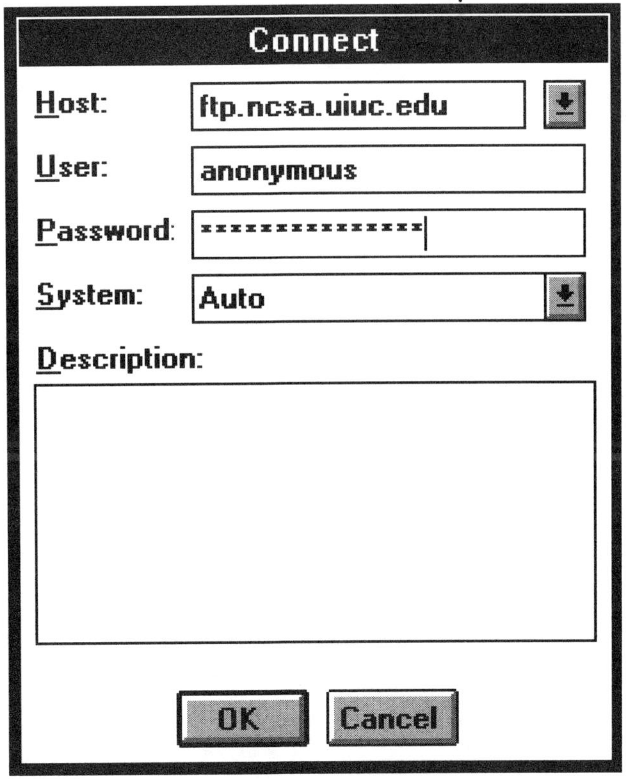

Figure 2-2: *A typical Connect dialog box.*

4. Type **anonymous** in the User name box.

5. For the password, enter your full Internet email address (username@site.domain). This is a common network convention used with FTP logins, hence the frequently used term "anonymous FTP."

6. Choose the OK button (or whatever the command is to establish the FTP connection).

7. Once connected, make your way through the directory hierarchy to the PC/Mosaic directory.

8. Once you've located the file wmos20a6r1.zip, transfer it to the Mosaic directory you created on your hard drive (following whatever instructions are appropriate for your FTP software—in the case of Chameleon FTP, you would select the left Copy button in the Files area of the FTP window).

9. Congratulations. You now have Mosaic on your hard drive. If you haven't already downloaded Win32s (and Trumpet Winsock, if needed), you can do so at this time. Win32s is located in the same directory. The file name is win32s11.zip. Trumpet Winsock is located the next subdirectory in /PC/Mosaic/sockets.

Due to the popularity of Mosaic, the NCSA sites handle huge amounts of traffic. To ease this traffic jam, try downloading Mosaic from one of the additional FTP sites found in Table 2-1 below.

Site Name	Directory Path
ftp.vmedia.com	/pub/companions/mosaicqt/ Windows/mosaic
sunsite.unc.edu	pub/packages/infosystems/WWW/ clients/Mosaic/Mosaic-NCSA/ Windows
miriworld.its.unimelb.edu.au	/pub/clients/PCmosaic
ftp.luth.se	/pub/infosystems/www/ncsa/ Windows
ftp.sunet.se	/pub/pc/Mosaic

Table 2-1: *Other FTP sites offering Mosaic.*

Mosaic has been widely distributed throughout the Internet. Besides the FTP sites above, many online services and other "islands in the Net" have it in their software libraries. Look around and download using whatever method you are most comfortable with.

The Ventana Visitors Center Ventana offers an Online Companion for the *Mosaic Quick Tour* as part of the Ventana Visitors Center. The Online Companion offers all the software mentioned in the *Quick Tour*, with the latest versions accessible as soon as they are made available, along with version change notes. There is also an online guide that will provide you with quick access to Internet resources related to this book. The Mosaic Quick Tour Online Companion will help make this book dynamic, up-to-date and continually useful.

The Ventana Visitors Center can be found at **http://www.vmedia.com/vvc/index.html**

The Mosaic Quick Tour Online Companion can be found at **http://www.vmedia.com/vvc/onlcomp/mosaicqtw/index.html**

- Check America Online, CompuServe or other services you may have access to.
  - The Ventana Visitors Center can be accessed as follows:

Gopher	gopher.vmedia.com
FTP	ftp.vmedia.com
WWW	http://www.vmedia.com/vvc
email	info@vmedia.com In body of message type **send help** (This will send more info about the center, *not* the Mosaic program itself.)

  - Art and Farces:

Gopher	gopher.farces.com
FTP	ftp.farces.com
WWW	http://www.farces.com/
email	almanac@farces.com In body of message type **send help** (This will send more info about the site, *not* the Mosaic program itself.)

  - Snail mailed from NCSA.

The National Center for Supercomputing Applications, creator and maintainer of Mosaic, has a catalog of software offerings, manuals and other information. You can get a copy via email or snail mail:

email	orders@ncsa.uiuc.edu
snail mail	NCSA Orders 152 Computing Applications Bldg. 605 East Springfield Ave. Champaign, IL 61820-5518

Unpacking Your Booty

Now that you have the necessary files transferred to your computer, you'll need to unpack them. The files come data compressed using a popular PC compression utility called PKZIP. To unzip them, you'll need PKUNZIP. The latest versions of PKZIP and PKUNZIP come bundled together as PKZ204G.EXE. The 204G is the current version; newer versions will have higher numerical designations. If you don't already have PKZ204G, you can get it via FTP from any of the sites listed in Table 2-2.

Site Name	Directory Path
bitsy.mit.edu	/pub/dos/utilities/pkz204g.exe
epas.utoronto.ca	/pub/pc/util/pkz204g.exe
gatekeeper.3com.com	/adapters/bin/pkz204g.exe
csuvax1.murdoch.edu.au	/pub/pc/pkz204g.exe

Table 2-2: *FTP sites offering the PKZIP utilities.*

Put PKZ204G.EXE in its own directory and make that your current directory. It is a self-extracting file, so all you need to do is run it and it unpacks itself. After you have PKZIP/PKUNZIP installed on your machine, you're ready to unpack everything else and put it in its proper place on your hard drive.

Note: It's a good idea to add the directory where PKUNZIP resides to your AUTOEXEC.BAT's path statement. That way, you won't have to tell your computer where the program is each time you wish to use it. You'll only need to type ***pkunzip -d [filename]*** *and it will do the rest (assuming the .zip file is already in the directory where you want the decompressed file to live). If you don't know how to modify the path in your AUTOEXEC.BAT file, shame on you (and consult your DOS manual).*

The basic procedure for unzipping files is simple.

1. Make the directory where you want the files to reside your current directory.

2. Choose Run from the Windows File menu.

3. Type **pkunzip -d filename.ext**. (such as wmos20a6r1.zip or win32s115.zip). Your files will be unpacked.

For further information on zipping and unzipping files, see the documentation that comes with PKZ204G. You can also see documentation by typing **pkunzip** without any parameters at the File/Run prompt.

Unpacking & Installing Win32s

When unpacking and installing Win32s,

1. Make sure you install the zipped Win32s files in the following subdirectory: \windows\system\win32s. Make this your current directory.

2. Choose Run from the Windows File menu.

3. The Win32s files come zipped in two subdirectories: \disk1 and \disk2. To make sure that the integrity of these directories is kept when you unzip the files, you need to use a -d switch in your unpacking command. So, the unzip command would look like this: pkunzip -d win32s115.zip.

4. Run the setup program in \disk1 and you should be all set. Read the readme file.

Unpacking & Installing Mosaic

When unpacking and installing Mosaic,

1. Start with the zipped Mosaic files in the Mosaic subdirectory on your hard drive.

2. From there, choose Run from the Windows File menu.

3. Type **pkunzip wmos20a6r1.zip** (or whatever the current version is called).

4. You should now have within that directory the following files:

mosaic.exe	The Mosaic program itself.
mosaic.ini	The initialization and configuration file. This should be copied (not moved) to your Windows directory.
install, update and readme .txt files	Text files with the basic info and latest update news on Mosaic.
faq.txt	The latest copy of Mosaic Frequently Asked Questions (with answers, of course).

One last thing before we move on to a basic configuration of Mosaic. Mosaic requires that your system has what's called a Winsock 1.1-compliant DLL (dynamic link library) installed. If you are using Chameleon or Trumpet Winsock, you should be all set. If you're using different TCP/IP software or are on a local area network, check with your network administrator and/or vendor to make sure you have the right Winsock DLL installed.

3W: The Internet With a Human Face

Magazines devoted to the Internet and computer communications used to be boring—technical, academic, drab—boring. A magazine from England called *3W: Global Networking Newsletter* has changed all that. Created by a group called Art + Computers, *3W* looks like a stylish print magazine that just happens to be about the Internet. *3W* avoids technical jargon, is geared toward all levels of users and doesn't talk down to new Net citizens. It takes an artful approach to computers while still managing to fill its pages with useful information. The magazine's motto, "The Internet with a Human Face," expresses its interest in the people part of the Internet equation rather than the technology. *3W* fosters a sense of "virtual community" on the Internet. Each issue includes listings of new sites, Net happenings and significant personalities. There are also articles on regional networks, BBSes and Internet administration. A WWW column contains descriptions and URLs of notable Web sites. If you want to stay plugged in (and still have a special place in your heart for high-quality print magazines), you may want to check out *3W*. For the latest subscription information, send email to 3W@ukartnet.demon.co.uk, or check their Web page at http://www.3W.com/3W/

Software	What It Does	Notes
PKZ204G	Compresses and decompresses files indicated by the .zip extension.	UNZIP is the utility required for unpacking the programs covered here.
TCP/IP protocol stack	Handles the data traffic between your PC and the Internet.	Chameleon NEWT and Trumpet Winsock are two examples.
Winsock.dll	Provides compatibility between different TCP/IP applications and the TCP/IP protocol stack.	Comes with some packages (such as the above). Can also be FTPed from NCSA and elsewhere.
Win32s	An upgrade for Windows 3.1 that is required to run 32-bit applications like Mosaic Alpha 6.	Needs to be installed as a subdirectory under your System subdirectory.
Mosaic 2.0 Alpha 6	The hypermedia browser we've all been waiting for.	Set it up in its own subdirectory. Read the text files that came with it.

Table 2-3: *The gnarly path to Mosaic. Carefully check to make sure you have all of these programs properly installed.*

Setting Basic Preferences

You could just launch Mosaic now, but in the interest of smoother sailing, there are a few things you might want to take care of first. The basic preferences for how you want Mosaic to look and behave are configured in what's called the mosaic.ini file. Here are some basic changes to make now. We'll look into the mosaic.ini file in more detail in Chapter 3.

1. The first thing you need to do is make a copy of the mosaic.ini file, which should now be located in your \Mosaic directory. Copy it (do not move it) to the \Windows directory.

Note: Alternately, you can tell your PC where to find the mosaic.ini file by adding it to your AUTOEXEC.BAT file, like this:

set MOSAIC.INI=c:\mosaic\mosaic.ini

(or whatever the exact directory path is on your system).

2. Open the mosaic.ini file using the Windows Notepad (or any text editor). The file will look like Figure 2-3.

The mosaic.ini file is divided by bracketed sections that define different aspects of Mosaic that are user configurable. The first series of changes you should make are in the [Main] section.

1. In the E-mail address entry, change it to E-mail= "username@site.domain" (with your user name and email address). This address will be used when/if you email the Mosaic developers using the "Mail to Developers" option under Mosaic's Help menu.

2. For the item "Autoload Home Page," set it to Autoload Home Page=no. If you leave it set to yes, your computer will automatically be logged into the Mosaic for Microsoft Windows Home Page at NCSA. You can save that site

Notepad - MOSAIC.INI
File Edit Search Help

```
[Main]
E-mail="user@site.domain"
Autoload Home Page=no
Home Page=http://www.ncsa.uiuc.edu/SDG/Software/WinMosaic/HomePage.html
Help Page=http://www.ncsa.uiuc.edu/SDG/Software/WinMosaic/Docs/WMosTOC.html
FAQ Page=http://www.ncsa.uiuc.edu/SDG/Software/WinMosaic/FAQ.html
Bug list=http://www.ncsa.uiuc.edu/SDG/Software/WinMosaic/Bugs.html
Feature Page=http://www.ncsa.uiuc.edu/SDG/Software/WinMosaic/Features.html
Display Inline Images=no
Dump memory blocks=yes
Grey Background=no
Fancy Rules=yes
Round List Bullets=yes
Current Hotlist=My Hotlists
Anchor Underline=no
Anchor Cursor=yes
Show URLs=yes
Extended FTP=yes
Toolbar=yes
Status bar=yes
Title/URL bar=yes
Use 8-bit Sound=no

[Settings]
Anchor Color=0,0,255


[Main Window]
x=0
y=-1
width=763
height=603

[Mail]
Default Title="WinMosaic auto-mail feedback"
```

Figure 2-3: *The mosaic.ini file.*

some unnecessary data traffic by setting this to no. In Chapter 3, I'll show you how to define a new home page.

3. If you're using a SLIP/PPP connection, you're going to want to set Display Inline Images=no. That way, when you go to a new page on the World Wide Web, if it includes inline images (graphics within the body of the page), they will not be loaded automatically. This will speed things up considerably. If you want to view any of the images, you can click on their inline image icon (with the right mouse button) and they will be opened.

4. Within the rest of the [Main] section it is recommended that for now Show URLs, Toolbar, Status bar and URL bar all be set to yes.

5. Under [Services], the NNTP (Network News Transport Protocol) Server should equal your network service provider's NNTP. This comes defaulted to the University of Illinois's NNTP server. If you have a local one, enter it here. It will usually be in the form of news.site.domain. This information should have come with your SLIP/PPP account.

6. The address for the SMTP (Simple Mail Transport Protocol) Server should be your local service's SMTP. This information also should have come with your SLIP/PPP account.

7. Save these changes to the mosaic.ini file. If you used something other than Notepad, make sure you save the file as text.

That's all the configuring you'll need to do in the mosaic.ini file to get you started.

Mosaic Quick Peek

Once you've established your network connection, double-click on the Mosaic icon (see Figure 2-4). If everything is properly set up, the program will launch and be ready to connect with your first Web document! Why not have a brief look around?

Figure 2-4: *Mosaic, your doorway to the Web.*

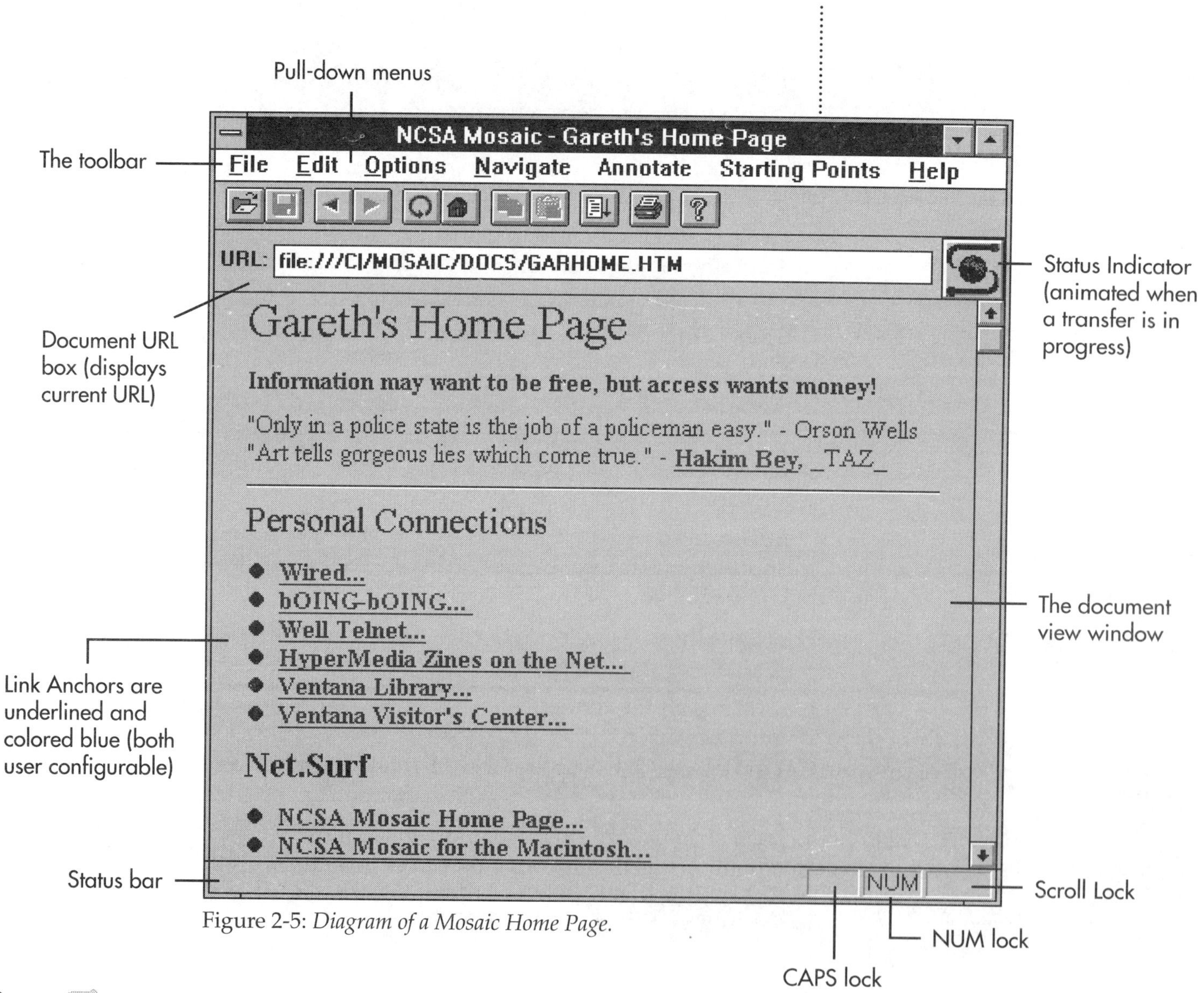

Figure 2-5: *Diagram of a Mosaic Home Page.*

Using URLs

Here are a few helpful pointers for the first-time Mosaic user.

1. The Document URL box lets you see the "address" of your current document location (it's blank at first if you've set the Autoload Home Page=no in the mosaic.ini file). You can type a new URL into the URL box and press Enter to connect with a Web location. (If you don't know any URLs, try http://www.vmedia.com. That's the URL for Ventana Online.) The Show Current URL feature should already be enabled if you entered it in the mosaic.ini file. If the Document URL box is not visible as shown in Figure 2-6, choose Show Current URL from the Options menu.

Figure 2-6: *The Document URL box.*

Note: URLs (or Uniform Resource Locators) are really the heart of Mosaic navigation. They are discussed in much greater detail in Chapter 3.

2. Similarly, the Show Status Bar option should also be defaulted to on. If not, select it from the Options menu. It allows you to monitor Mosaic's actions. The Status bar is located in the lower left-hand corner of the Mosaic screen. (See Figure 2-7.)

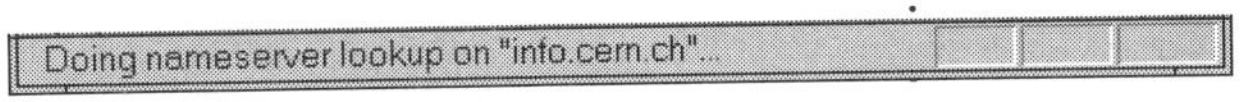

Figure 2-7: *The Status bar.*

3. Finally, you should have turned Display Inline Images off in the mosaic.ini file. Check on this by looking under Options and making sure the Display Inline Images item is not checked. Now, when Mosaic encounters an inline image (a graphic within a Mosaic document), it will only display an icon that indicates there's an image available. To view any of these images, simply click on the icon using the right mouse button and the image will be loaded. If you're using Mosaic over a SLIP/PPP connection, you want to have this option turned off. Otherwise, you may have to go out and run around the block a few times or take a nap every time you connect to a site with large and frequent inline images.

Figure 2-8: *Inline Image icon.*

HOT TIP

If your PC is on a dedicated network connection, such as a campus or corporate LAN, you can leave the Display Inline Image feature on. Because you have a much higher transfer rate, the images won't take that long to load.

Having a Look Around

Now...finally...you're ready to give Mosaic a real whirl. Log onto any of the Web pages listed in the Starting Points menu item. There are plenty of resources there to keep you busy. Try clicking on some of the hyperlinked anchors (items underlined and shown in blue). Wander, explore, have some fun!

You can use the Back and Forward arrow icons (located in the toolbar) to move back and forth through documents you have already loaded. The Forward arrow only works if you've moved back a document (or more) and then want to go forward again. The Back arrow takes you to the previous document. See Figure 2-9. The Home button will only work if you have a URL specified as home. We'll go over how to set up a new home page in Chapter 3.

Note: We have not yet configured the Helper Applications that Mosaic uses to view large images and movies and to play sounds (which are set up in the [Viewers] section of the mosaic.ini file). How to do this is covered in Chapter 3. For purposes of this quick peek, don't click on any anchors that are hyperlinked to images, movies or sounds.

Figure 2-9: *The navigation buttons.*

Roadside America in the Web! The authors of the Roadside America series of wacky travel guides (most recently *New Roadside America*, Simon & Schuster, 1992) hit the road again, this time taking the Internet with them. *Hypertour '94* authors Mike Wilkins, Doug Kirby and Ken Smith logged some 4,000 miles in seven days, between June 29 and July 5, 1994. They let the Internet follow their exploits by uploading daily reports and images to *Wired* magazine's Web site and to the Wired forum on America Online. They dispatched daily travel logs, photos and even QuickTime movies of their trip, stuffing all this data through the phone lines of their hotel →

If you need any roadside assistance, check out the NCSA for Microsoft Windows Home Page (http://www.ncsa.uiuc.edu/SDG/Software/WinMosaic/HomePage.html) for links to online documentation and look under Mosaic's Help menu.

rooms each night. Always true to their bizarre and playful curiosities, they stopped at such places as Beaver, Oklahoma, the "Cow Chip Throwing Capital of the World"; the pint-sized Stonehenge replica in Rolla, Missouri; Philippi, West Virginia, home of the West Virginia Mummies; New Vrindeban, a Krishna palace and theme park (also in West Virginia); and the creepy Mutter Museum of preserved medical oddities in Philadelphia (where the thorax of John Wilkes Booth is preserved).

Internetters were also able to send messages to the group and get personal responses by posting messages on America Online. The trio of authors have became America's foremost authorities on out-of-the-way and unusual tourist attractions, having traveled some 100,000 miles over the years in search of the unique, the forgotten and the strange.

The archives of *Hypertour '94* are located at http://www.wired.com and in the Wired forum on America Online (keyword: wired).

Moving On

Now that you've learned a little bit about Mosaic and have spent some time in Webspace, you've probably caught a glimpse of why everyone seems so excited. Mosaic adds a whole new level of ease and flexibility to navigating cyberspace—and God knows, today's cyberspace needs that.

The next chapter is intended to move, step by step, through Mosaic's basic features. Again, you probably don't have to read it all (although you know what Mom would say!). If you're feeling brave and want to learn as you go, you can jump back into Webspace with this guide in hand and then look things up when you get stuck.

3

Cruising Mosaic's Menus

Never worry about theory as long as the machinery does what it's supposed to do.
— R. A. Heinlein

Mosaic is not a difficult program to learn. Part of its popularity is due to its familiar graphic interface and its intuitive workings. While the basics of Mosaic are easily mastered, even its more technical and esoteric aspects are approachable by most Net citizens.

This chapter covers each feature of Mosaic and gives a brief introduction to all of its menus and each item found within those menus. Before we begin our menu tour, to ensure a smooth ride through Mosaic, be sure to finish configuring your preferences (see "Setting Basic Preferences" on page 24).

When our tour of Mosaic's menus is done you'll want to

- Check to make sure you have all the Helper Applications you'll need to view graphics and movies and to hear audio clips (see "Configuring Helper Applications" on page 61).

- Learn enough about how fonts and styles work in Mosaic so that you can control the look of your Web documents (see page 65).
- Make sure that you know how the Custom Menus/Hotlists feature works (see pages 68-74).

Mosaic's Menus

Let's take a trip through Mosaic's menus to see how everything works. After you've had a brief look around, you can decide where you want to return and spend more time.

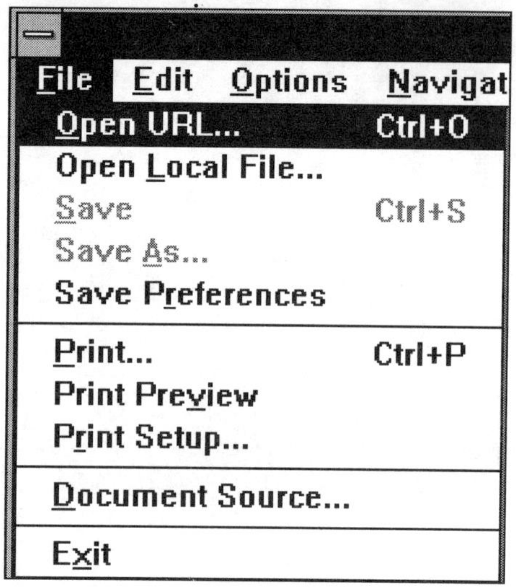

Figure 3-1: *Mosaic's File menu.*

The File Menu

If you are familiar with the Windows environment, you already know many of the functions found under the Mosaic File menu. It is here that you open documents, save and print documents, and exit Mosaic.

Open URL...

One of the main tools used for moving from one Web page to another is the Open URL window. After selecting this feature, a window appears (see Figure 3-2) with a box for entering a Uniform Resource Locator (URL). URLs are the addresses for documents accessible through the World Wide Web. You can either type in the URL (in the upper left box) or cut and paste it from another source. Clicking OK begins the connection to the site where that document is located. An Open URL button is also available on the toolbar. For complete information on URLs and how they work, see "What Is a URL?" on page 78.

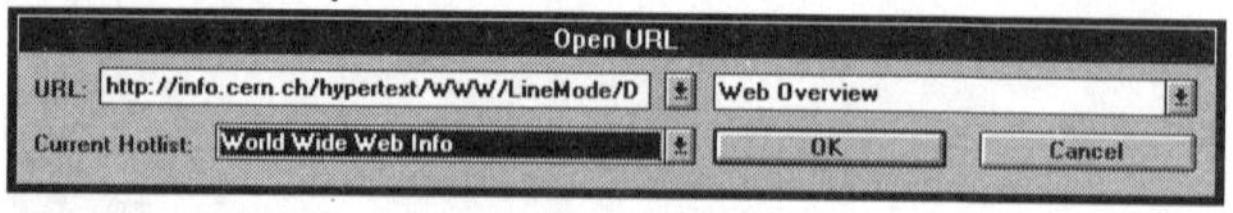

Figure 3-2: *The Open URL window.*

Note: There are two other ways of entering URLs. You can enter them in the URL box located above the Mosaic document view window (if you have Show Current URL selected in the Options menu) or you can click on the Open URL icon on the toolbar (assuming you have the toolbar selected in Options). The URL icon is the open file folder at the far left of the bar. See pages 74–76 for a full description of the toolbar and its contents.

The Open URL window also displays the currently selected hotlist (in the lower left-hand box). The box in the upper right displays the name of the currently selected document. By clicking on the Down arrow of any of these three boxes, you can select a new URL, document or hotlist. To change the current hotlist (more on hotlists below), simply select the new list in the Current Hotlist box and then click Cancel. That way, the next time you invoke the Open URL window (or choose Add Current To Hotlist from the Navigate menu), your newly selected list will be current. To actually go to the Web documents listed in the hotlists, select the desired document (which will be named in the upper right-hand box) and then click on OK (or choose Enter). Mosaic will make the connection to the Web site where that document is located.

Open Local File...

Allows you to open a local (on your hard drive) HyperText Markup Language (HTML) or text document. Open Local File is also useful for testing your homemade Web documents before you unleash them on the rest of the world. (See Chapter 4 for making your own HTML documents.)

Save

Saves the currently viewed document to your hard drive.

Save As...

Allows you to save the current Mosaic document in 3 different flavors: as plain text, in HTML format or as a binary file. If you save a document as plain text, all HTML information will be stripped from it. This is similar to word processed documents formatted as ASCII text. All graphic elements, type styles (bold, underline), etc., will be removed. Saving a document as HTML writes it to your hard drive as an HTML document with all *link anchors* (links to other documents), *tags* (the actual HTML codes), URLs and other formatting information intact. This information is the "source code" of HTML.

Save Preferences

Saves the currently configured screen dimensions and the current state of items selected (or deselected) under the Options menu.

Print...

Presents print options in a standard Print dialog box. Prints the full contents of the current document (including material above and/or below the Mosaic document window). If you want the printing to be the same as what you see in Mosaic, you must have scalable versions of the fonts installed on your system. Check font selections (and change as needed) in the Choose Font section of the Options menu. A Print button is also available on the toolbar.

Print Preview

Displays a copy of the document as it will be printed.

Print Setup...

Presents a standard Windows Print Setup dialog box.

> *Note: There is a glitch in Mosaic Alpha 6. Both the Preferences and Print Setup quick key combinations use the r key. This will be fixed in the next version.*

Document Source...

Opens an HTML version of the document you are currently viewing. Opening up and viewing HTML documents found on the World Wide Web is a great way to learn about how these documents are created. Document Source will only open up HTML and plain text documents (from your hard drive). It will not open FTP and Gopher directories.

Choosing Document Source will take you to a separate window with its own menu. The choices here are:

- *File...Save:* Saves the document that is displayed in the Document Source window to your hard drive. The document must be saved with the .htm extension. This is the HTML extension translated for a DOS environment.
- *File...Exit:* Closes the Document Source window and returns you to the main Mosaic window.
- *Edit...Copy:* If you click and drag selected text from the Document Source window, Copy will copy it to the Clipboard for later pasting.

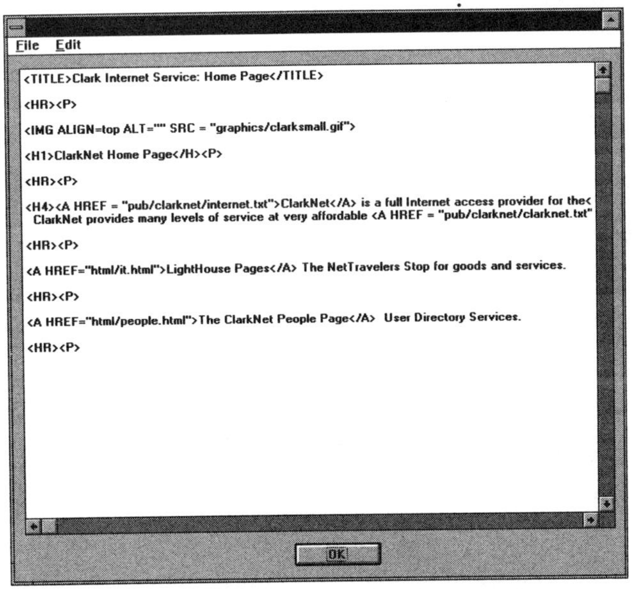

Figure 3-3: *The Document Source window.*

You can also click on the OK button (or press Enter) located at the bottom of the Document Source window to return to the main Mosaic window.

Note: If you have problems getting the Document Source window to display the current HTML document, close the Document Source window. Return to the document you want to send to the Document Source window and select Reload (either from the toolbar or the Navigate menu). After the document has been redrawn, return to the Document Source window and you should now see the tagged HTML document.

Exit

Now I don't have to tell you what that does, do I?

The Edit Menu

The Edit menu choices in Mosaic for Windows are short and sweet: Copy and Find... that's all you get.

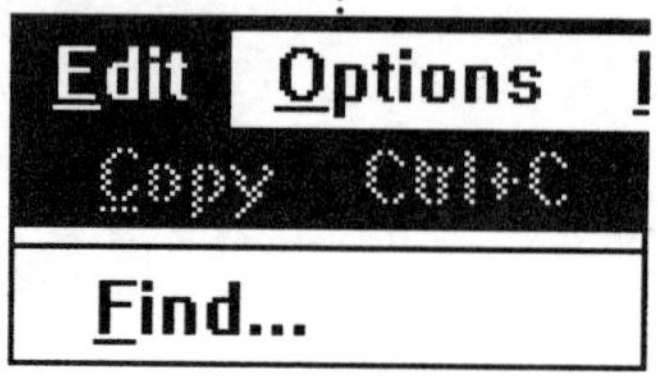

Figure 3-4: *Mosaic's Edit menu.*

Copy

Copies selected text. You can copy text from any of the data entry boxes, URL boxes and from the Document Source window. At this time, you cannot copy material from Web documents. Hopefully the NCSA developers will implement this in the future (the Mac version already allows it). For now, you can use the Save As command under the File menu to save text documents to disk. A Copy button is also available on the toolbar.

Find...

Locates text within the currently displayed document. A window pops up asking "Find What:". See Figure 3-5.

A check box within the Find window offers a Match Case search option. This will match the upper- and lowercase of the text string being searched. For example, with this option selected, a search on "Table" will not find "table." Press the Find Next button to go to each occurrence of the word or text string. A Find button is also available on the toolbar.

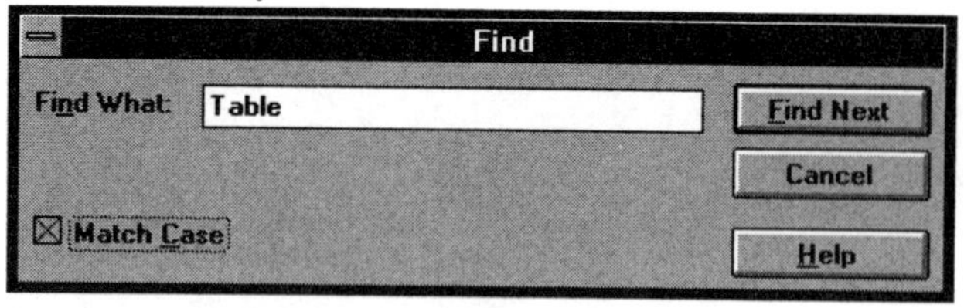

Figure 3-5: *The Mosaic Find window.*

HOT TIP

Is it a box or is it a window? The difference between a dialog box and a window can sometimes be confusing. In *Mosaic Quick Tour*, the following distinctions are made:

- *Windows* are pop-up screens that can be moved around, opened or closed, overlapped, and placed behind and on top of other windows. Multiple windows can be open at the same time.
- *Dialog boxes* cannot be moved and they will not go away until you interact with them (e.g., entering information or pressing a button). A dialog-type box that is non-interactive (doesn't ask you to do anything) is called a *Message box* (e.g., "HTAccess: Error Accessing").

HOT TIP

Make sure that when you quit your Mosaic sessions, you disconnect your Internet connection. Just exiting Mosaic will not automatically disconnect you. This can be a problem; you can stay connected for hours before noticing (I know from experience). Some services automatically break your connection if it remains idle for a certain amount of time. Others don't. Regardless, the best thing to do is to keep the connection window for your TCP/IP software visible and remember to disconnect after leaving Mosaic (unless you're planning on using another TCP/IP application).

The Options Menu

The Options menu in Mosaic is one of the most useful menus in the program. It offers several monitoring functions for Web navigation (Current URL and Status displays) and is used when displaying and moving documents (Load to Disk, Display Inline Images). It's also where you access the Font windows, which are important for altering the look of your Web documents.

Load to Disk

When checked, tells Mosaic to load documents to disk as you access them. If you've selected this option, whenever you open a new document, either by clicking on a link anchor or by selecting Open URL, Mosaic brings up a Save As dialog box instead of displaying the document. You select where you want the transferred file to be placed on your hard drive. This option is useful if you want to retrieve, say, an MPEG movie, and you want to keep it rather than have Mosaic temporarily store it, show it, and then dump it when you quit. When you're done using Load to Disk, remember to turn it off in the Options menu. Otherwise, the Save As dialog box will pop up every time you select something. A Load to Disk button is also available on the toolbar but is not yet implemented.

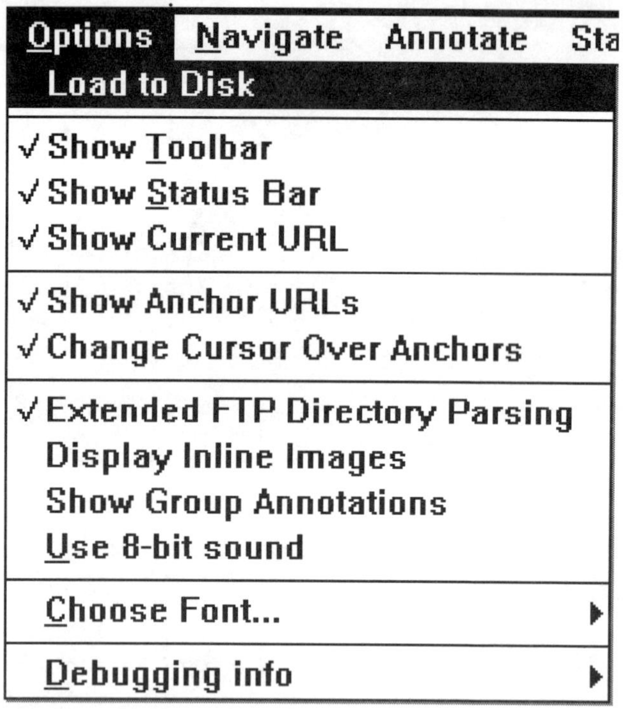

Figure 3-6: *The Options menu.*

HOT TIP

You can also invoke the Load to Disk command using your mouse. Simply put the finger cursor over the link anchor of the item you want to load, hold down the Shift key and then click the left mouse button. The Save As dialog box appears. After you've saved the particular file to disk, you do not have to de-select Load to Disk from the menu. Using the mouse approach only loads the single file. It does not "turn on" the Load to Disk feature.

HOT TIP

When saving files to disk, remember to check their file names, keeping in mind that Windows is going to use only the first eight characters before the extension and only the first three characters of the extension (for instance, all .html documents become .htm documents). In the Save As dialog box, you can rename the file something more sensible if the truncated eight-character name is going to render it senseless.

Show Toolbar

When this option is checked, the toolbar is displayed along the top of the main Mosaic window (just below the menu items). See a full explanation of the toolbar on page 74.

Figure 3-7: *The Mosaic toolbar.*

Show Status Bar

Displays the area for status messages located in the bottom-left corner of the main Mosaic window. Status messages let you know what Web document is currently being looked for, when a connection is being made, the status of the document's transfer, etc.

Figure 3-8: *The Status bar.*

Show Current URL

Turns the URL display box on and off in the main Mosaic window. When this is turned off, the Status Indicator (the NCSA logo) is also removed from the Mosaic window.

Figure 3-9: *The Document URL box and Status Indicator.*

Show Anchor URLs

When this item is selected, moving the pointing finger cursor over a link anchor causes the Status bar to display the URL for that link.

Change Cursor Over Anchors

Keep this option checked if you want the arrow cursor to switch to the pointing finger cursor whenever a hyperlinked item is encountered.

Extended FTP Directory Parsing

Selecting this item will display cute little file icons whenever you arrive at an FTP site. When this option is not selected, the FTP site will display only drab and dreary file names and directories (and who wants that?).

Display Inline Images

Automatically loads inline images when you open a document that contains them. This dramatically slows down access time over a dial-up SLIP or PPP connection. If Display Inline Images does not have a check-mark by it, it is turned off and the inline image icons will be displayed in the document window (indicating that an inline image exists).

Inline image icon

To view inline images, simply click on the icon using the right mouse button. The image will be transferred and displayed in the document window. If it's a hyperlinked inline icon, indicated by a border in the anchor color, you can

1. View the inline image first by clicking the right mouse button.

2. Go directly to the hyperlinked item by clicking the left mouse button (the inline image will not be displayed).

Show Group Annotations

In Mosaic for Windows 2.x, you can share annotations over a work group. To enable this feature, this item must be checked. See the section on the Annotate menu below.

Note: You must also have the server name for your local area network specified in the mosaic.ini file to make use of group annotations.

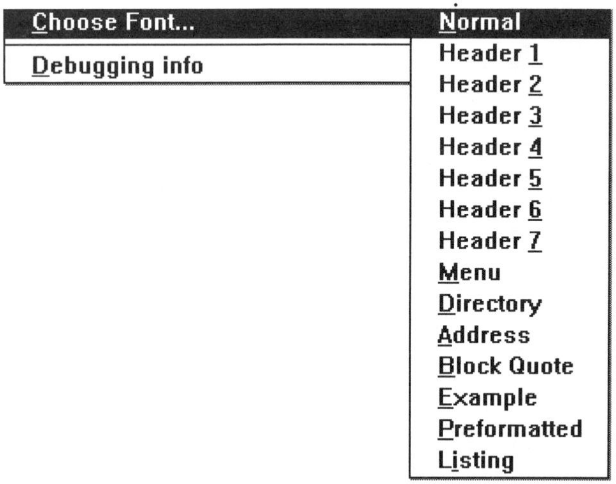

Figure 3-10: *The Choose Font... submenu.*

Use 8-bit Sound

With this checked, all sound files that you transfer in Mosaic will be handled by an 8-bit sound card. This is useful if you don't have a 16-bit card installed.

Choose Font...

Selecting this item presents you with a submenu of style types you can alter in Mosaic's document view window. See the section on "Using Styles in Mosaic" later in this chapter.

Debugging info

A submenu offering a series of alerts and warning messages that can be toggled on and off when this item is selected. This menu is for developers only and is not for average Mosaic use.

The Navigate Menu

Mosaic includes many menu, command key and iconographic options for navigating the Web. The Navigate menu (see Figure 3-11) offers many of the same features found on the toolbar.

Back

Lets you move back through the documents you've visited most recently. Back stays dimmed until you have a previous page to return to. A Back button is also available on the toolbar.

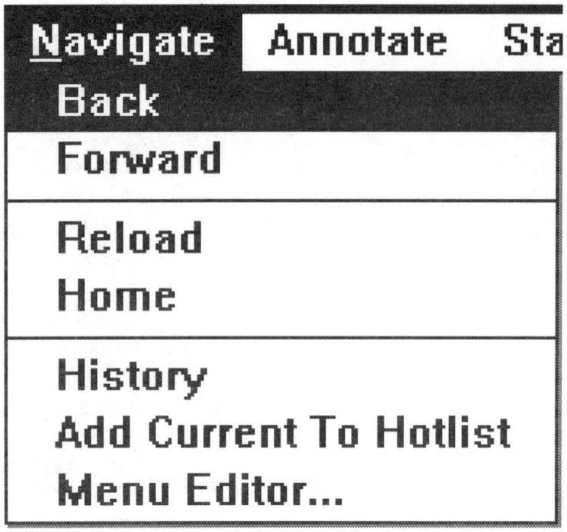

Figure 3-11: *The Navigate menu.*

Forward

Lets you move forward through the pages you've visited during your current Mosaic session. Only works if you have been back through pages and then decided to move forward again. Stays dimmed until you have a forward page to move to. A Forward button is also available on the toolbar.

Reload

Causes the current Web page to be redrawn in the document view window. Some sites also use the Reload command as a way of loading a series of pictures. Instead of going to several Web pages to view a succession of images, you stay on one page and select Reload to see new images. Reload is also used when you make changes in or delete an annotation and you want the changes to take effect immediately. A Reload button is also available on the toolbar.

Home

Takes you back to your home page, which, if you're using the defaulted home page, is the NCSA server. Home can be a comforting place to return to if you get hopelessly tangled in Webspace. A Home button is also available on the toolbar. See Chapter 4 for instructions on building your own snazzy home pages.

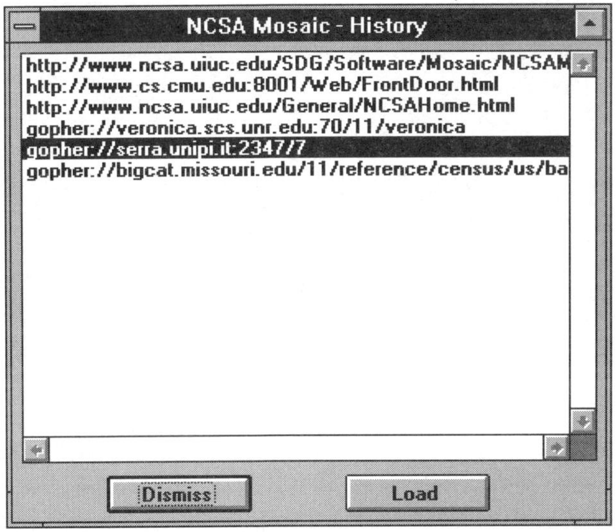

Figure 3-12: *The History window.*

History

A list of the documents you have visited during your current Mosaic session is available here. To return to a site previously visited and stored in History,

1. Click on the History menu item. A window will appear containing a list of recently viewed documents. See Figure 3-12.

2. The currently selected Web document will be highlighted. Using the mouse, select the site that you want to return to and click the Load button. You can also double-click on the site name. Either way, Mosaic will begin its attempt at accessing that site.

3. When you are done viewing the History window, choose Dismiss. If you load a previous site, the window closes automatically after the document has loaded.

Notice that the History window is a scrollable field. You can scroll up and down to select other sites that may not be visible in the window.

Add Current To Hotlist

Adds the currently displayed document's name and URL to your currently selected hotlist. To change the current hotlist,

1. Choose Open URL from the File menu (or from the toolbar).

2. Press on the arrow in the Current Hotlist box located in the lower left-hand corner of the Open URL window. A pull-down menu will appear showing all your hotlists.

3. Select the list that you want to start using as your new hotlist.

4. Instead of clicking on OK (which would load the first document in the list), choose Cancel. The hotlist that's visible in the Current Hotlist box when you cancel will become the new list. From now on, when you choose Add Current To Hotlist while at a Web document, that document's name and URL will be added to the end of the currently selected list.

Lost in the Tangle of Hypertext? History in hypermedia is very important. Studies done early in the development of hypertext found that people had a hard time staying "connected" to their thought process if they got lost in a hypertangle of information. Encouraging self-exploration is a great benefit of hypertext/hypermedia, but that needs to be balanced with a sense of logical organization. Being able to see where you've been and to move back to previous branching off points is very important. In Mosaic, the History window and the Back, Forward and Home buttons help you keep track of where you've been and the documents you've browsed along the way.

Menu Editor...

Allows you to build custom pull-down menus and submenus. This selection will take you to the Menu Editor where you can delete, add or change custom menus of document titles/URLs. See the "Creating Custom Hotlist Menus" section later in this chapter for the lowdown on this useful and flexible feature of Mosaic for Windows.

> *Note: All changes to the Menu Editor should be done here, not in the mosaic.ini file.*

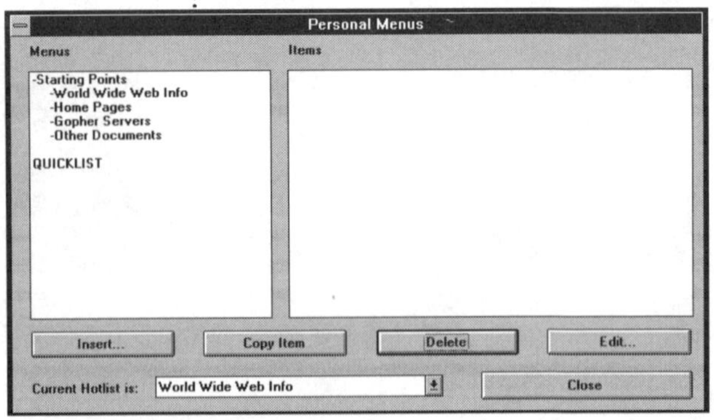

Figure 3-13: *The Menu Editor window.*

The Annotate Menu

Lets you access written annotations, personal Post-it notes, that you can attach to a Web document.

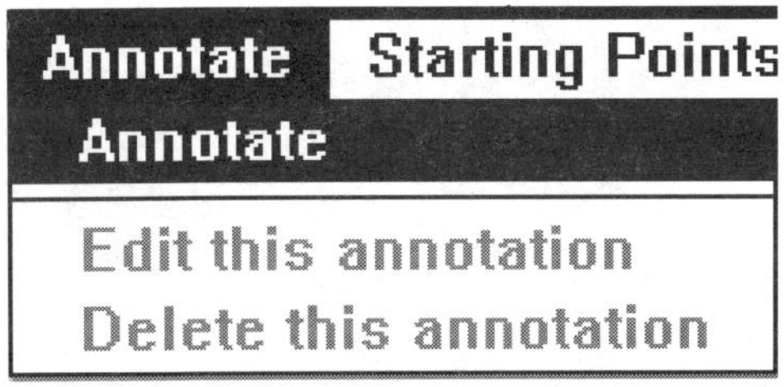

Figure 3-14: *The Annotate menu.*

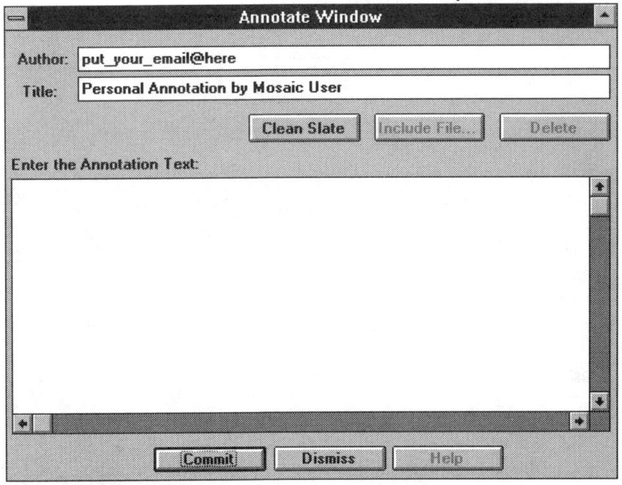

Figure 3-15: *The Annotate window.*

Annotate

Opens an Annotate window (see Figure 3-15), allowing you to attach personal notes to the Web page currently being viewed. Your email address (if you entered it in the mosaic.ini file) automatically appears in the Author box.

To add an annotation,

1. Select Annotate from the Annotate menu.

2. In the Annotate window, enter a new name in the Author box if you don't want to use your defaulted email address.

3. Enter a title for your note in the Title box.

4. Type your note in the scrollable text box provided.

5. When your note is complete, click Commit.

6. The annotation will not take effect until the next time this page is loaded into the Mosaic document view window. If you want it to take effect immediately, choose Reload from the Navigate menu (or from the toolbar). The words *Personal Annotations* will appear at the end of the document, indicating that this page has a note attached to it.

Note: NCSA plans on adding an audio annotation to a future version of Mosaic.

To view an annotation,

1. When you encounter a Web page that includes annotations, you will see the words Personal Annotations at the very bottom of the page. To view your notes, choose Annotate from the Annotate menu.

2. When you're done reading the annotations, choose Dismiss from the Annotate window.

Other features of the Annotate window include:

- *Clean Slate:* Deletes the current contents of the Annotate text field.
- *Include File:* When implemented, this feature allows you to attach a text file to your annotations. This does not work in Mosaic Alpha 6.
- *Delete:* Allows you to highlight and delete selected text from your annotations. This is not working on Alpha 6. For now, if you want to delete text, you have to insert the cursor and use the Backspace key.
- *Help:* Not yet implemented. Will present onscreen assistant in using the Annotate feature.

Edit this annotation

Allows editing of text annotations. This command brings up the original annotation. Once you've made your text changes, choose Reload from the Navigate menu (or the Reload button on the toolbar) and the changes will take effect immediately.

Do-It-Yourself Electronic Publishing The Internet is not only a great place to engage in stimulating conversations and to consume news and information, it can also turn you into a news and information producer. Thousands of Net citizens publish their own electronic newsletters, moderated mailing lists, FAQs and Web documents.

Brock N. Meeks, by day a writer for *Communications Daily*, becomes a one-man wire service by night. He is the creator of *CyberWire Dispatch,* a series of erratically published reports on significant Net happenings, communications law and policy, and freedom of speech issues in cyberspace. Meeks's service is free and his dispatches are serious, in-depth and hard-hitting. *CyberWire Dispatch* has been mentioned in a number of magazines and dailies, including *The New York Times, The Washington Post* and *Wired* magazine. The *Dispatch* can be delivered directly to your email box by sending mail to majordomo@cyberwerks.com with "subscribe cwd-l" as the first line of your message. To access *CyberWire Dispatch* on the Web, send a URL to http://cyberwerks.com:70/1/cyberwire. Back issues are available in gopherspace from gopher cyberwerks.com. →

Delete this annotation

Allows you to delete annotations. The deletion will not take effect immediately. The words Personal Annotation will continue to appear on the page until the next time Mosaic downloads this document. If you want the deletion to take effect immediately, select Reload from the Navigate menu (or the Reload button on the toolbar).

Note: Annotations are personal and cannot be accessed by anyone else on the Internet. They are stored on your hard drive and are not made part of the HTML documents you are viewing. Mosaic for Windows does allow you to share annotations over a workgroup. Unfortunately, you can only have group or personal annotations in documents, not both.

Jon Lebkowsky and Paco Xander Nathan, both well-known Net personalities, are quickly becoming mini-media moguls. Several years ago, they started FringeWare, a company and Net community dedicated to creating an alternative marketplace for goods and services offered by Net citizens. They now maintain a conference on the WELL BBS, publish a Net-based catalog, moderate a mailing list on alternative community and do-it-yourself technology, and publish two print magazines: *FringeWare Review* and *Unshaved Truths*. And—if that wasn't enough—they have day jobs! The FringeWare Home Page is located at http://io.com/commercial/fringeware/home.html

These are just two examples of successful Net-based publishing efforts. There are countless others. As you delve deeper into the Web, you'll find many new and exciting forms of media.

Starting Points

This menu is your gateway to some of the most useful resources on the Internet. From here you can easily access the various Web pages at NCSA, other university sites, Gopherspace, the Finger and Whois gateways and an Archie server. If you have read this *Quick Tour* and are ready to do some serious Web walking, this is an excellent place to start. The following table lists the items available under the Starting Points menu and what they offer.

Menu Item	Offering
Starting Points	A hyperlinked reference page containing numerous key Internet resources. Contains most of the resources listed below (and a lot more).
NCSA Mosaic Demo Document	Provides an interactive tour of Mosaic's capabilities.
NCSA What's New Page	Opens NCSA's frequently updated list of news and new offerings on the Web.
NCSA Mosaic Home Page	Connects you to the home page of the Web server at NCSA.
Windows Mosaic Home Page	The official entry point and information center for the Microsoft Windows version of Mosaic.
World Wide Web Info	Includes a subdirectory of information on the WWW and a series of searchable Web directories. A great place to get an broad overview of Web offerings.
Home Pages	Instant links to the front doors of 21 university Web sites.
Gopher Servers	Gateways to eight Gopher information servers including the popular Veronica and the original Gopher at UMN. Also includes a comprehensive directory of all the Gophers in the world.
Finger Gateway	Provides a URL connection to the Finger Gateway at the University of Indiana. Finger is a UNIX-based utility that can be used to search email and biographical information about people on UNIX networks.
Whois Gateway	Whois allows you to search for people in cyberspace.
Other Documents	A brief listing of other interesting Net points. This hotlist is also a good place to add your own hotlist items until you learn how to create your own.
Archie Request Form	A form-based Archie gateway for the WWW. Lets you access a series of Archie servers throughout the world.

Table 3-1: *Starting Points on the World Wide Web.*

Note: The Starting Points menu is completely user-configurable. You can add/change/edit however you like. See the section below on "Creating Custom Hotlist Menus" for more information. Also keep in mind that Mosaic is freeware and is passed through the Net by many hands. The version you download may have different items added or subtracted from the above list. This just means that an individual loaded a copy to a Net site that they had already customized. If the additions/changes are acceptable, no problem. If you suspect that your copy of Mosaic has been monkeyed with in a disagreeable way, try getting a new copy from a different site.

The Help Menu

The contents of the Help menu are only accessable if you are Net connected. These files are not stored on your machine, they are located at NCSA. See Figure 3-16.

Online Documentation

Contains an online user's guide prepared by the developers at NCSA.

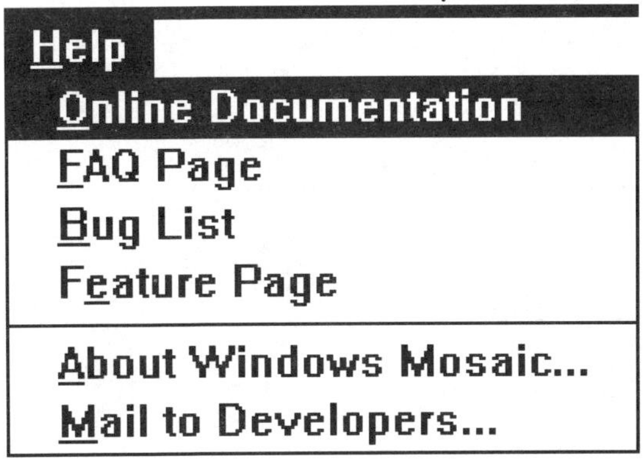

Figure 3-16: *The Help menu.*

FAQ Page

Takes you to a series of Frequently Asked Questions about Mosaic for Windows.

Bug List

An up-to-date listing of the known bugs (and bug-like features) in the current version of Mosaic.

Feature Page

A history of the features of the various versions of Mosaic for Windows.

About Windows Mosaic...

A standard "About..." program identification box listing version number, copyright information, developers' names and the email address at NCSA.

Mail to Developers...

Allows you to send an email message to the software developers at NCSA. When chosen, a window pops up with the email address of NCSA hardwired in. If you've entered your email address in the mosaic.ini file, all you have to do is enter the subject of your message in the Subject box and the text of your message in the scrolling text box. When you're done, click Send, and your pithy prose will be posted to NCSA.

Two important things to remember:

1. Before you can send this email message, you must enter your return email address on the E-mail= line in the mosaic.ini file. If you haven't done that, you can still use this option by manually entering the address of your email account in the appropriate box (as username@site.domain).

2. Since Mosaic does not support other forms of email besides this outgoing message to the developers, you need to have a regular Internet address to receive an answer.

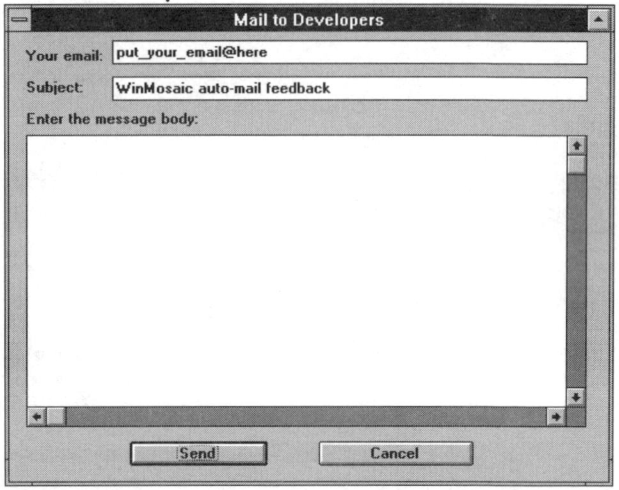

Figure 3-17: *The Mail to Developers window.*

As you might imagine, the developers at NCSA get a lot of mail from Mosaic users. Please don't take advantage of this service. Before you send your question(s), make sure you've looked through *Mosaic Quick Tour*, in the online Mosaic help documents and at the various Mosaic and WWW FAQs (Frequently Asked Questions) files.

Note: It's a shame that the NCSA address cannot be changed in this window. If it could, then this feature could be used as an outgoing mail box to anyone on the Net. If you'd like to be able to send and receive email during your Mosaic sessions, you can use programs such as Eudora. See Chapter 4 for more information.

Configuring Preferences

You enter your preferences here for how you want Mosaic to behave in the mosaic.ini file. (You should have already copied (not moved) the mosaic.ini file from your Mosaic directory to the Windows directory.) When editing this mosaic.ini file it's probably a good idea not to be running Mosaic (OK...call me superstitious).

To open the mosaic.ini file, use the Windows Notepad or any text editor or word processing program. You will see that the mosaic.ini file is divided into a series of subsections. Let's run through them section by section and examine what they contain.

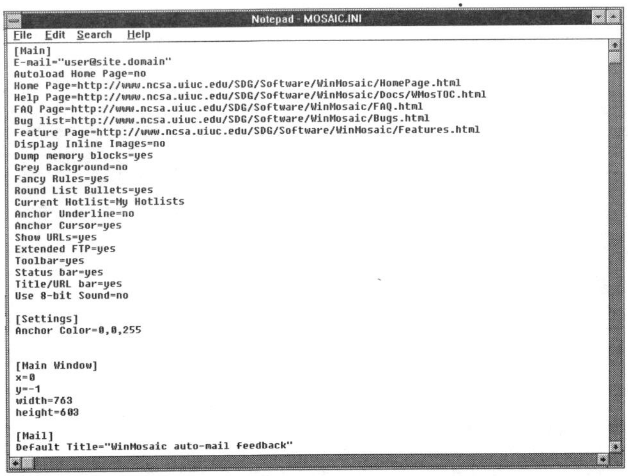


```
[Main]
E-mail="user@site.domain"
Autoload Home Page=no
Home Page=http://www.ncsa.uiuc.edu/SDG/Software/WinMosaic/HomePage.html
Help Page=http://www.ncsa.uiuc.edu/SDG/Software/WinMosaic/Docs/WMosTOC.html
FAQ Page=http://www.ncsa.uiuc.edu/SDG/Software/WinMosaic/FAQ.html
Bug list=http://www.ncsa.uiuc.edu/SDG/Software/WinMosaic/Bugs.html
Feature Page=http://www.ncsa.uiuc.edu/SDG/Software/WinMosaic/Features.html
Display Inline Images=no
Dump memory blocks=yes
Grey Background=no
Fancy Rules=yes
Round List Bullets=yes
Current Hotlist=My Hotlists
Anchor Underline=no
Anchor Cursor=yes
Show URLs=yes
Extended FTP=yes
Toolbar=yes
Status bar=yes
Title/URL bar=yes
Use 8-bit Sound=no

[Settings]
Anchor Color=0,0,255


[Main Window]
x=0
y=-1
width=763
height=603

[Mail]
Default Title="WinMosaic auto-mail feedback"
```

Figure 3-18: *The [Main] section of the mosaic.ini file.*

[Main]

This section contains identification information for your email address and your Home Page. There are also a number of display options. See Figure 3-18.

E-mail=[email address here]

By adding your email address between the quotation marks, you are telling Mosaic where you want it to return any email messages that you send to the developers at NCSA (using the Mail to Developers option in the Help menu). This address will also be defaulted as the "Author" of your personal annotations. Enter your address in the standard form of username@site.domain.

Autoload Home Page=

Setting this to yes will cause the Home Page URL listed below to be loaded whenever you launch Mosaic. If you don't want a page loaded automatically, set this to no.

Home Page=[URL here]

This is the Web-based or local drive-based HTML document that you want Mosaic to access each time you open the program. If you don't want Mosaic to load any home page, you still need to set Autoload Home Page to no. (Just deleting the URL here would not be enough.) The Home Page URL is usually defaulted to the server at NCSA.

If you decide to use an HTML document on your hard drive as the default Home Page, you'll need to use the following URL form: file:///c|/directory/filepathname.

The Help Page=, FAQ Page=, Bug List= and Feature Page= are all URLs that are accessed by Mosaic for use in the Help menu. Do not change these (unless one of the URLs becomes obsolete).

Display Inline Images=

If this item is set to yes, each time you access a Web document that contains graphics, Mosaic will automatically load the graphics after loading the text. For slower connections (SLIP/PPP), it is recommended that you have this set to no. This way you can save the time of waiting for all the inlines to load. After the page is loaded you can then decide which images you want to view. To load them, click on the inline image icon with the right mouse button.

Dump memory blocks=

This is something that was added to Alpha 6 and will not appear in future versions. Ignore it.

Grey Background=

If set to yes, the NCSA document view window will have a grey background (the same shade of grey as the panel above the document window). If set to no, the document view window will be white.

> **Why Do You Think They Call It "Mosaic"?**
> At this point you've probably realized that Mosaic for Windows is a pretty cool program. But, you may also be wondering where its name came from. Why is a World Wide Web browser named after a type of art that combines different pieces of material (such as glass or tile) to create complex designs? Well—that's exactly what Mosaic does. Rather than having to reinvent the wheel every time a new multimedia format is introduced, it assembles Web hypermedia using external programs that are all put together in Mosaic. Because Mosaic uses this open, plug-in approach, it can remain flexible as new media forms enter cyberspace. New animation formats (QuickTime VR, for example)? No problem. Just define a new MIME type, map it to the appropriate viewer application and Mosaic is ready to display QuickTime VR. New sound format? Just configure the sound program, point Mosaic to it in the mosaic.ini file and off you go. Mosaic takes all these pieces and puts them together into a multimedia—well—*mosaic!*

Fancy Rules=

If set to yes, a fancier type of rule will appear in HTML documents tagged with an <h> (in HyperText Markup Language).

Round List Bullets=

Allows you to replace round bullets in bulleted lists with little flat line markers. This saves load time if this option is set to no.

Current Hotlist=[Hotlist name here]

Entering the name of a hotlist here will make that list the current list each time you return to Mosaic. You can make other lists the Current Hotlist during your Mosaic sessions, but each time you return, the list entered above will be defaulted.

Anchor Underline=

Link anchors (or hyperlinks) are shown in a color in Windows Mosaic (defaulted to blue). If you also want all links to be underlined, set this item to yes.

Note: It's a good idea to use Anchor Underlining if you're using Mosaic with a monochrome or grayscale monitor. Otherwise, link anchors will not be obvious to you until you drag the cursor over them (assuming you have Anchor Cursor set to yes).

Anchor Cursor=

By setting this to yes, the standard Windows arrow cursor will change to a pointing finger cursor whenever the cursor moves over a link anchor. Isn't the little hand cute? Well, it's functional anyway.

Note: Anchor Colors are called Hotlinks in Mosaic for Mac and X Windows. On all platforms they are also referred to frequently as hyperlinks.

Show URLs=

If turned on, URL addresses will appear in the Status bar (assuming you have that set to yes) whenever the cursor moves over a link anchor.

Extended FTP=

When you encounter an FTP or Gopher site in Mosaic, you have options as to what you see. If set to yes, the site displays icons relevant to the type of file being viewed. If the size of the file has been specified you will see that too. If this option is set to no, you see only a list of directories and files with no icons and no file size indications.

Toolbar=

The toolbar that runs along the top of the main Mosaic window is one of the most important navigation tools in the program. If you want the displaying of the toolbar to be defaulted, set this to yes.

Status bar=

The Status bar, located in the lower left-hand corner of the main Mosaic window, gives you valuable feedback as to what Mosaic is up to at any given time (during file access and transfer). Vote yes, if you want this bar to always appear (unless you toggle it off in the Options menu).

Title URL bar=

This option, set to yes, will display the URL bar and Status Indicator (NCSA logo) at the top of the document view window.

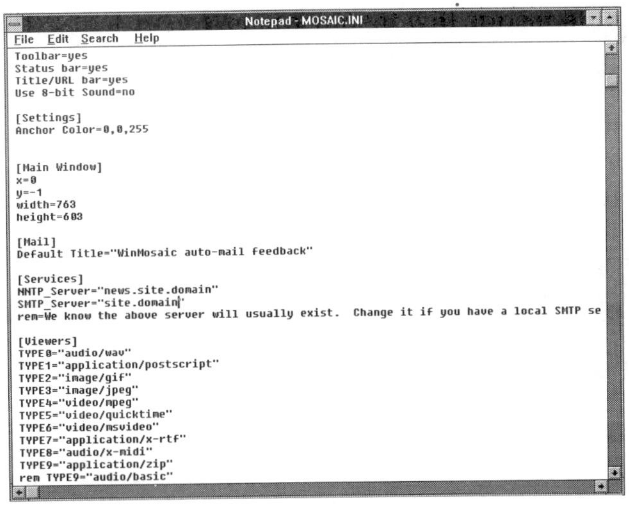

Figure 3-19: *More of the mosaic.ini file.*

Use 8-bit Sound

With this checked, all sound files that you transfer in Mosaic will be handled by an 8-bit sound card. This is useful if you don't have a 16-bit card installed.

[Settings]

Here is where you specify what color you want Mosaic link anchors to be. The default color is blue (0,0,255). The color values are expressed as numbers with zero being no instance of the color and 255 being full strength. The color value sequence is red, green, blue. If you wanted to change the anchor color to red, you would change the setting here to 255,0,0. Green would be 0,255,0 and so forth.

[Main Window]

The Main Window refers to the size of the main Mosaic window and its position on your monitor. Do not edit this directly in the mosaic.ini file. To change the screen size and location,

1. From within Mosaic, resize the main window to your desired configuration and move it on the screen where you want it to appear each time it's launched.

2. Choose Save Preferences from the File menu and the window size and position will be written to the mosaic.ini file.

Note: If you have made any other changes in preferences from within Mosaic (such as Display Inline Images, Show Status Bar, Show URLs, etc.), these changes will also be saved to the mosaic.ini file and will become the default preferences. If you do not want this to happen, make sure you only change the window size/position before selecting the Save Preferences option.

[Mail]

When you choose Mail to Developers in the Help menu from within Mosaic, what you have entered here will always appear as the default title of your message. You can, of course, change that title for each instance to reflect the current subject of the message. The mail title comes defaulted to "WinMosaic auto-mail feedback." If you want it defaulted to something else, say "Fanmail from Some Flounder" or "HELP!!!!!," you can make those changes here. Your return email address also needs to be entered in the appropriate line above (in the [Main] section) if you want NCSA to be able to respond to your question. Also, if you have a local SMTP server (at your Internet service provider's site, for instance), make sure that is changed in the [Services] section below.

[Services]

To be able to read USENET Newsgroups from within Mosaic and to get responses to email messages sent to NCSA, you need this section to be properly filled out.

- *NNTP Server=:* The NNTP (Network News Transport Protocol) server should equal your network service provider's NNTP. Mosaic comes defaulted to the University of Illinois's NNTP server (news.cso.uiuc.edu). This will work fine as a newsgroup gateway, but to save traffic to this site, if you have a local NNTP server, enter it here. It will usually be in the form of "news.site.domain." This information should have come with your SLIP/PPP account.

Note: On some Internet service providers' set-up information sheets, this address is also called an NNRP instead of NNTP. This probably stands for Network News Reader Protocol.

- *SMTP Server=:* The address for the SMTP (Simple Mail Transport Protocol) server should be your local service's SMTP. Mosaic comes defaulted to the NCSA's NNTP server (ftp.ncsa.uiuc.edu). This will work as a mail gateway, but to save traffic to this site, if you have a local SMTP server, enter it here. This information should have also come with your SLIP/PPP account.

Figure 3-20: *The [Viewers] section of the mosaic.ini file.*

[Viewers]

Viewers (or Helper Applications) are external programs that Mosaic uses to access media files (sounds, graphics, movies) on the Web. It is in this section of the mosaic.ini file where you can "map" Helper Application types to specific applications and then define the local hard drive directory path to those applications. That way, when Mosaic encounters a file of that media type, it will transfer the file, hold it temporarily and then launch the external application to show or play the media file in question. See "Configuring Helper Applications" below for more detailed instructions on using these external applications with Mosaic.

[Suffixes]

Suffixes refer to the file extensions that Mosaic looks for in accessed media files. These suffixes only come into play on FTP sites and Web sites using HTTP version 0.9. These 0.9 sites are very rare and you will probably not encounter them. HTTP version 1.0 does not use these suffixes because the file is typed by the server and not your Mosaic client. For each file type, you can list as many different versions of the extension as you think Mosaic may encounter. For instance,

image/jeg=.jpeg,.jpg.,jpe
video/quicktime=.mov,.moov (and so forth)

Make sure that the extension list is separated by commas (no space) and that each extension begins with a period (.).

[Annotations]

In Mosaic 2.x, annotations can be personal or shared over a workgroup. Your personal annotations are stored within a file on your PC, while group annotations are stored on a local networked machine. Here is where you define the storage location for personal and group annotations.

- *Directory="c:\mosaic\annotate":* (or whatever the directory path is on your machine).
- *Default Title="Personal Annotation by Mosaic User":* If you want a different title to appear when your choose an annotation, enter it here. The obvious choice would be to replace Mosaic User with your name.
- *Group Annotations=:* If you are planning on sharing annotations over a network, set this to yes. Otherwise, leave it defaulted to no. You can also toggle this on and off by checking Show Group Annotations under the Options menu.

- *Group Annotation Server="your.local.lan.server:portNumber":* To share annotations over a local network you need to specify the machine on the network (and the port number) where the group annotations will be stored. Check with your LAN administrator for more information.

[User Menu#]

This section of the mosaic.ini file shows you the structure and contents of your user-configurable hotlist menus. Do not change them here. If you want to create, add to or change menus, use the Menu Editor found under Navigate within Mosaic. See "Creating Custom Hotlist Menus" below for more information.

[HotList]

This section is a list of URLs that are contained in the Quicklist. The Quicklist is a general hotlist that comes already set up with Mosaic. Using the Menu Editor, you can add and subtract to this list as you please. The Quicklist is the only hotlist that is not part of the Starting Points pull-down menu. You access Quicklist via the Open URL window. To edit the Quicklist (or any hotlist), use the Menu Editor. Do not, however, change anything in this area of the mosaic.ini file.

[Document Caching]

Type=Number
Number=[#]

Document Caching refers to how many documents Mosaic will store. Each time you load a Web document to your screen, that document will go into the cache (up to the number you specify here). If you then return to one of the documents that's been cached, Mosaic doesn't need to reload it from its server. So, as you might imagine, the best thing to do is to select a high number to save time and unnecessary Net traffic.

How many documents you specify is a function of how much memory your PC has. If you have a large amount of RAM, select a higher number, if you're low on RAM, select only a few cached documents. If you're really pushing your available memory, set this number to zero (no caching). You can experiment to find a number that's appropriate. A good number to start with is 5.

[Font] sections

Again, this area of the mosaic.ini file is not to be changed. All changes to fonts and font styles are done in the Choose Font choice under the Options menu.

[Proxy Information]

Your copy of the mosaic.ini file may include a section on Proxy Firewall services (or a section can be added if appropriate). A proxy service processes network input and output to and from computers on a local area network (LAN) that sits behind a firewall (a computer security barrier that prevents unwanted intrusions). By gatewaying through a proxy service, the LAN can pretend that it's actually on the Net when (technically) it isn't (it's being mediated through the proxy). For full details on using a proxy service with Mosaic, check out the document at **http://www.ncsa.uiuc.edu/SDG/Software/WinMosaic/ProxyInfo.html**

What in Blue Blazes Is a Firewall? A firewall is a server computer that is set up between the users of a local area network (or LAN) and their gateway to the Internet. As you might imagine, because the Internet is public, it's not very secure. Every computer on the Internet is considered a peer of every other computer. A computer attached to a LAN that is routed to the Internet is potentially accessible to anyone on the Net. A firewall processes network input and output and allows the computers on a LAN to pretend that they're actually on the Net when they (technically) aren't. The problem with this scheme is that it sometimes hinders the performance of programs that want to be directly Net-connected. Mosaic is such a program. The CERN Proxy/SOCKS services, now available with Mosaic 2.x, help improve gateway performance for systems that are hiding behind firewalls.

Configuring Helper Applications

Helper Applications are external programs that Mosaic uses to help it display various media files. This scheme allows Mosaic to keep its mind on its business, while letting other sophisticated viewing and listening applications handle the media presentations. This also gives Mosaic a great degree of flexibility, allowing you to add new types of Helper Applications as you need them.

The first thing you need to do is check to see which of the Helper Applications you have and which you'll need. Table 3-2 shows you the main default applications Mosaic uses.

File Type	Default Application	Special Requirements	Payment Type
GIF/JPEG (images)	LView	SVGA Monitor	Freeware
QuickTime (movies)	Movie Player	QuickTime For Windows	Freeware
MPEG (movies)	MPEGPLAY	8mb Ram Recommended	Shareware
AU (sounds)	WHAM (w/sound card)	Sound Card	Donationware
AU (sounds)	WPlany (w/o sound card)	PC Speaker Driver (speak.exe)	Freeware
Zip (compressed files)	PKUNZIP	(None)	Shareware

Table 3-2: *The default Helper Applications.*

All of these programs are freeware or shareware and are available via anonymous FTP from many of the FTP sites listed elsewhere in this book. (See Table 2-2 in Chapter 2 for FTP site listings.)

Before you've downloaded the Helper Applications you need, you should create a home directory for them. If you're truly lazy, you can look at each Helper Application in the mosaic.ini file and find out what the defaulted pathname is, creating the appropriate directories to conform to those paths. This way, you won't have to change any filepaths in the mosaic.ini file. A more sensible approach would be,

1. On your hard drive, create a directory called apps (or whatever you wish to call it). Mine is c:\windows\apps.

2. Within the new apps directory, create a new subdirectory for each application (c:\windows\apps\mpegplay, c:\windows\apps\lview, c:\windows\apps\wplany, etc.).

3. Download (or move within your hard drive) the zipped Helper Application files into their respective subdirectories. See Chapter 2 for information on FTPing files.

4. Unzip the files in their respective subdirectories.

5. Read each app's installation instructions, registrations and readme files.

6. Open up the mosaic.ini file using the Windows Notepad. Within the [Viewers] section of the mosaic.ini file, find the pathname for each Helper Application. Change the path to reflect its location on your drive. In our example, we would make sure that each path read

"c:\windows\apps\helper_app_name.%ls"

7. Save the mosaic.ini file.

That should be all there is to it (assuming you've followed any instructions that came with the application). Now, when you encounter a media file during a Mosaic session and download it, Mosaic will access the appropriate helper and use it to open the file. When done viewing or listening, you can quit the Helper Application (which is now on top of Mosaic) or you can save the file to disk, if that option is available.

If you wish to change any of the Helper Applications or add new applications, you'll need to go back in the mosaic.ini file.

For example, let's say you want to change an application. Mosaic is defaulted to access LView as the application for displaying jpeg images. If you didn't have LView, but have another graphics application, such as Photoshop, here's how you would configure Mosaic to use the new application:

1. First, determine the filepath of the new application. In this case it's c:\photoshp\photoshp.exe (or whatever the pathname might be).

2. Open up the mosaic.ini file using Notepad and find the image/jpeg= application line.

3. Change the current jpeg= statement to equal the pathname of your new application (in this case, image/jpeg= "c:\photoshp\photoshp %ls"). Notice that the extension .exe was dropped and the argument %ls was added.

Note: Notice the forward slashes used in MIME typing as opposed to the DOS backslashes. Be careful when editing Helper Applications that you slash forward and back at the right time. It can get confusing.

4. Save the changes to the mosaic.ini file.

5. Launch Mosaic and retrieve a copy of whatever file will require that Helper Application type (for our example, we would want to find a jpeg image to view).

6. If your test is unsuccessful, go back to the mosaic.ini file and make sure you have the pathname correct. Also look in the top section of [Viewers], in the part that has Type[x]=, to make sure that the application you're attempting to "map" has a MIME type listed (more on MIME types below).

```
image/gif="c:\windows\apps\lview\lview31 %ls"
image/jpeg="c:\windows\apps\lview\lview31 %ls"
video/mpeg="c:\win32app\mpegplay\mpegplay %ls"
```

Figure 3-21: *Changing a Helper Application.*

```
image/gif="c:\windows\apps\lview\lview31 %ls"
image/jpeg="c:\photoshp\photoshp %ls"
video/mpeg="c:\win32app\mpegplay\megplay %ls"
```

Figure 3-22: *The new Helper Application for JPEG images.*

Mapping New File Types

The other main feature of the [Viewers] section of the mosaic.ini file is the ability to add new types of files and to "map" them to applications found on your hard drive. The first part of the [Viewers] section is a listing of many of the MIME file types that Mosaic recognizes. MIME (or Multi-purpose Internet Mail Extensions) is a standard originally developed for attaching media messages to conventional Internet email. Mosaic has adopted this standard and uses MIME file types for specifying its external Helper Applications. Table 3-3 shows the common file types that Mosaic recognizes and the defaulted applications (if any).

File Type	Subtype	Application
Text	plain text	Notepad
	richtext	MS Write
	html	Mosaic
Audio	basic	Mosaic
	wav	WHAM
	wav	Media Player
	x-midi	Media Player
Images	jpeg	LView
	gif	LView
	tiff	(no default application)
	x-xbm	(no default application)
Video	mpeg	MPEGPLAY
	quicktime	Movie Player
	msvideo	Media Player
Applications	postscript	Ghostview
	zip	UnZip

Table 3-3: *Common files types and Helper Applications in Mosaic.*

HOT TIP

The first time you launch Mosaic, you automatically go the Mosaic Home Page at NCSA. Due to the current popularity of Mosaic, traffic to the NCSA server is high. You can ease this burden on the electronic highways by making another Web location the default home page. Simply change the Home Page= line in the mosaic.ini file. I suggest you choose Ventana's Visitors Center at **http://www.vmedia.com/vvc** as your new Home Page. That way, you can keep up with the latest news about Mosaic and the Web, this book, and the newest releases of all the freeware and shareware covered here. Once you've entered the new Home Page URL, save the changes to the mosaic.ini file and relaunch Mosaic.

Using Styles in Mosaic

The Choose Font feature (found under the Options menu) allows you to customize the look of the Web documents you view. The documents you view in Mosaic are created using HTML "tags," sometimes called "style tags." These are bracketed codes that tell Mosaic how to display the various parts of a document. The information that's communicated over the Web does not specify the actual font, it simply tells Mosaic what style category to present things as (normal paragraph, top level header, a quotation, etc.). You get to choose the actual font and style in which the document will appear. Here's where you get to be a little creative—changing styles and font sizes to suit your fancy. See Table 3-4 for a list of the different parts of an HTML document and what changing them will affect.

Style Type	What It Modifies
Normal	The default paragraph style.
Header 1	Topmost heading.
Header 2	Second level heading.
Header 3	Third level heading.
Header 4	Fourth level heading.
Header 5	Fifth level heading.
Header 6	Sixth level heading.
Header 7	Seventh level heading.
Menu	List in menu form.
Directory	List in directory form.
Address	How the author's name and email address will appear at the bottom of documents.
Blockquote	Extended or block quotations.
Example	Short samples of code.
Preformatted	Text already formatted in monospaced font (e.g., program listings).
Listing	Long instances of code samples.

Table 3-4: *Paragraph style tags that can be modified in Mosaic.*

To change any of the default type styles in Mosaic,

1. Pull down the Options menu and click on Choose Font. A submenu will appear. See Figure 3-23.

2. Select the paragraph style you want to change (see Table 3-4 if you are unsure what some of these styles represent).

3. A Font selection window will pop up offering you a list of the fonts in your system to choose from, a font style (regular, italic, bold, bold italic) and a list of font sizes.

4. Choose the combination you want (remember, you are just changing the part of the paragraph you selected in step 2, not the entire document). The Sample box displays the characteristics (font, style, size) of your choice.

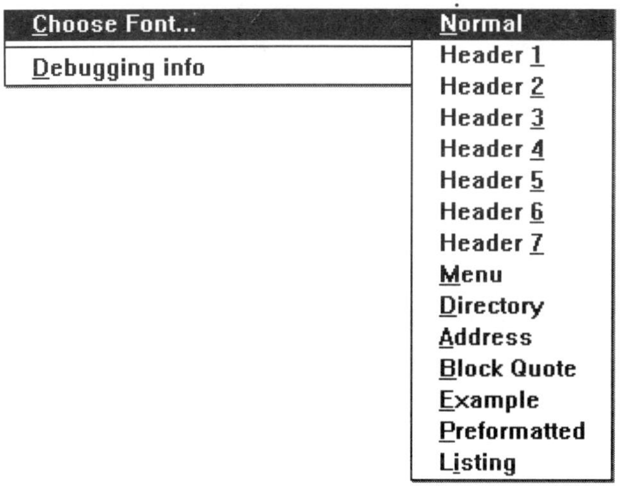

Figure 3-23: *The Choose Font... menu.*

5. When you are happy with your selection, click on the OK button.

6. You should see your changes in the current Web document you are viewing. These changes do not just affect this document but all future documents until you change the Font settings again.

Let's try a few more examples to make this clearer.

If you want all information that's been tagged within an HTML document as the style Blockquote to always appear in boldface 24-point Times, you would select Blockquote in the Choose Font menu, and make those selections in the Font window. From then on, whenever a document appears that includes blockquotes, it will appear on your Web document as boldface 24-point Times.

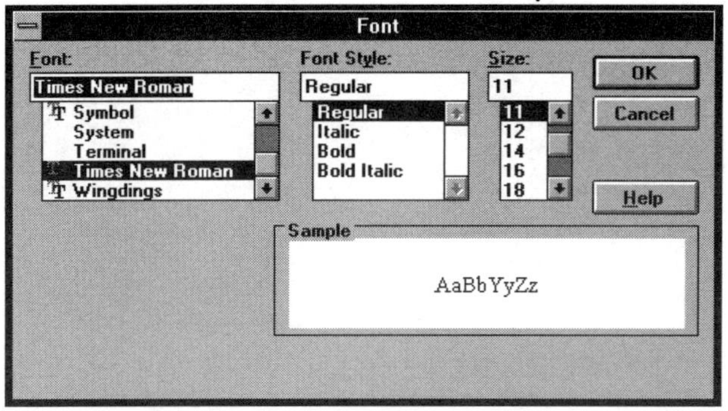

Figure 3-24: *The Font window.*

Keep in mind that these changes will only effect styles that have been appropriately tagged by the document's creator. If an HTML document creator decides not to tag an address with the HTML tags that specify an address, your choosing a special font or style for addresses will have no effect on that particular document. It should also be clear that the changes you make do not affect that actual HTML document—just the way your copy of Mosaic presents it to you.

Using Forms

The introduction and increasing sophistication of forms in HTML documents is one of the things that has excited people so much about the growth of Mosaic. Before forms, the World Wide Web was only a document viewing environment. The ability to enter information into boxes on a Web page makes the World Wide Web now a two-way means of communication. Some of the ways that forms can be used are outlined in Table 3-5.

If you are interested in learning more about forms and how to create forms using HTML, check out the Web document located at **http://south.ncsa.uiuc.edu/forms.html**.

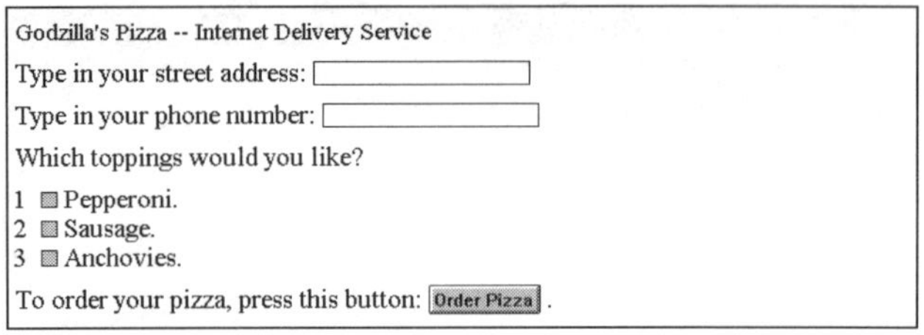

Figure 3-25: *A typical form in a Web document.*

How to Use Hotlists

There are so many great resources to discover in the Web. In an average Mosaic session you can open up oodles of documents, explore dozens of hyperlinks and generally tangle yourself up into knots. One of the most useful features of Mosaic is Hotlists, the feature that enables you to create multiple "address books" of documents you've visited that you might want to return to. You can save these lists under different names and even exchange lists with other Mosaic users.

Creating Your First Hotlist

The easiest way to get started with hotlists is to use the Quicklist that comes already set up in Mosaic. Although this list already contains some URLs, you can delete them if you like or just start adding to this list, using it as your current hotlist. To do this,

1. Select the Open URL item from the File menu.

2. When the Open URL window pops up, choose the Quicklist from among the lists offered under the Current Hotlist box.

Form Type	Usage
Ordering	Commerce on the Net. Allows Net-based shoppers to select items from online catalogs. Credit card information can also be taken and is becoming increasingly secure thanks to digital signature and encryption technology.
Survey	Web users are now able to fill out all types of information for commercial, government and private purposes.
Database	The ability to handle multiple forms and check boxes allows for even greater levels of sophistication and flexibility in searching databases for online information.
Feedback	Sites can now let users give direct input without having to resort to email.
Interactive Talk	Form-based discussion groups similar to USENET Newsgroups.
Password	Forms can be used to create private Web sites that can only be entered with a password.
Gaming	All variety of so-called rotisserie games (baseball, football) and other form-based games are possible using Mosaic's form features.
Free Expression	A number of sites on the Web use forms as a way of letting people input poetry, ideas, graffiti and other creative forms of expression.

Table 3-5: *Common uses for forms.*

3. With the Quicklist visible in the Current Hotlist box, choose Cancel. This Quicklist will now be considered your current hotlist.

4. Whenever you come to a Web site that you want to add to the Quicklist, choose Add Current To Hotlist from the Navigate menu. Your new Web document will appear at the bottom of the list.

Creating Custom Hotlist Menus

Before we create our first hotlist menu from scratch, let's open up the Menu Editor located under the Navigate menu. The Menu Editor window will appear. See Figure 3-26.

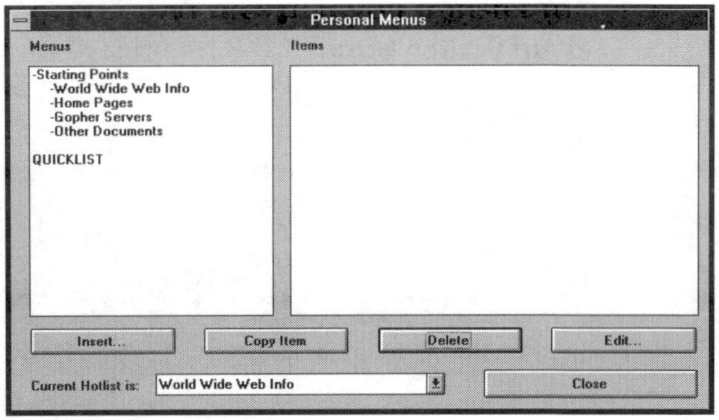

Figure 3-26: *The Menu Editor window.*

The Menu Editor

You will see two fields within this window. The left field, the Menus field, contains a list of all the user-configured menus currently set up in Mosaic. The right field contains the items from each one of the menus as you select them in the Menus field.

Insert...

This button opens the Add Item window. Here you can enter a new item into an existing menu, add a submenu to an existing top-level menu or create a new top-level menu.

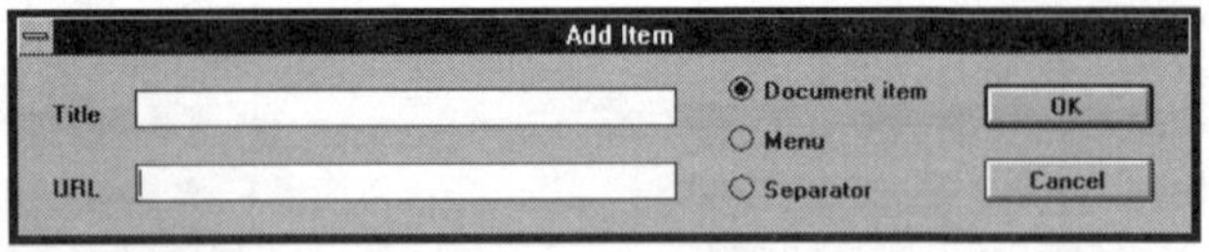

Figure 3-27: *The Add Item window.*

If you want to insert an item somewhere in a list, click on the menu item *below* where you want your item inserted. If you want to add the item to the end of the existing list, you don't need to specify a location, and it will automatically be added to the bottom of the list.

The Add Item window always opens up with the currently selected document displayed in its Title and URL field. If that is not the document you wish to add to your list, you can enter in a new title and URL. If you want to copy an item from another menu list, go to that item in the Menu Editor, select the Copy Item button (see below for more info) and then return to the Add Item menu (by rechoosing Add Item). Your newly selected list's name and URL will appear in the appropriate boxes.

There are three buttons on the Add Item window.

- *Document Item:* Adds a title and URL to an existing menu.
- *Menu*: Creates a new menu with the title specified in the Title box.
- *Separator:* Adds a line into a pull-down menu if you want the menu to have several separated subsections.

Copy Item

Clicking this button from the Menu Editor copies the document title and URL to memory. The next time you open the Add Item window, this document will appear as the selected title/URL.

Delete

Removes the document or entire menu that you've selected. You will get a dialog box asking if you really want to do this. Make sure you are deleting the right thing. The Quicklist menu item cannot be deleted, although items within it can.

Edit...

Choosing this item causes the Edit Item window to appear. From here you can edit the name of a menu and the contents of menus. You cannot rename the Quicklist. It is hardwired into Mosaic. You can, however, edit its contents.

Now that we know what everything does, let's create a new hotlist menu. Since I want to have a series of my own hotlists easily accessible, I want to create a top-level menu that will appear as a pull-down menu in Mosaic's main window. That way, I can add items and submenus as I choose.

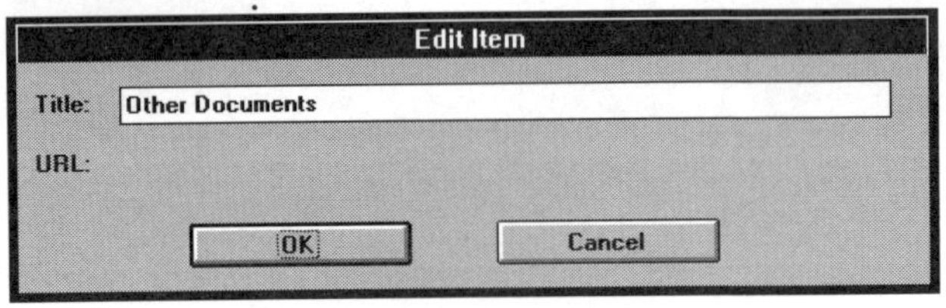

Figure 3-28: *The Edit Item window.*

1. Open the Menu Editor again (from the Navigate menu).
2. Highlight the empty space right above QUICKLIST in the Menus field (the left-hand field). You will notice when you do this that the right-hand field (Items) will display the statement "Click 'Insert' to add a toplevel menu."
3. Click on the Insert button and the Add Item window will appear.
4. Since we're creating a top-level menu, only the Title box is available. Notice also that the Menu radio button is the only selection available. Enter a title for this menu, "My Hotlists," for instance.
5. When you've entered the title, choose OK.
6. You will be returned to the Menu Editor, where you should see your new menu in the list of top-level menus. See Figure 3-30.
7. From the Menu Editor you can now select your new menu and begin adding document titles and URLs (or you can select the new menu as your Current Hotlist and then start building the list as you travel through cyberspace). Remember, you can either add documents directly to this top-level menu or create submenus within it (see below).

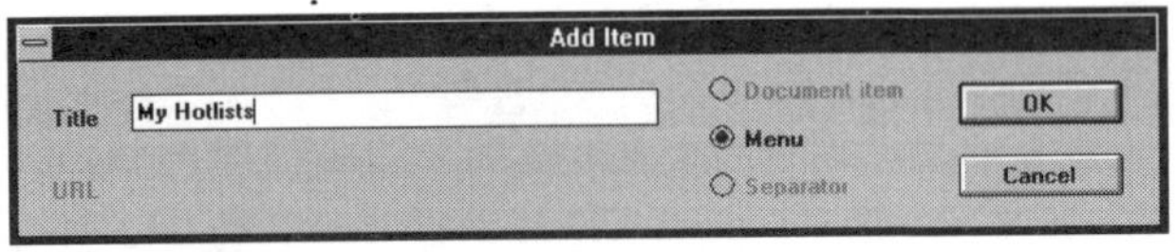

Figure 3-29: *Creating a hotlist menu.*

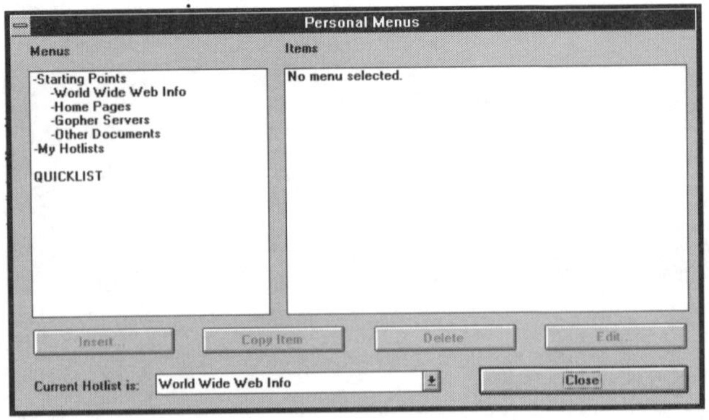

Figure 3-30: *The new top-level hotlist menu.*

Adding a Submenu

Adding a submenu to an existing top-level menu is easy.

1. Go to the Menu Editor and highlight the top-level menu you wish to add a submenu to. In this case I want to add the submenu Art and Design to My Hotlists.

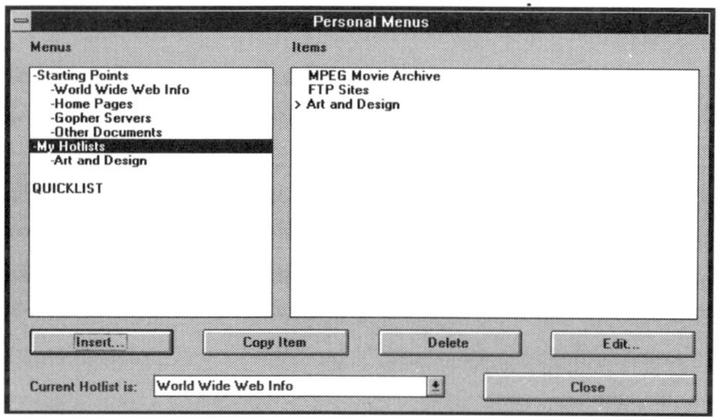

Figure 3-31: *The new hotlist submenu for Art and Design.*

2. With My Hotlists highlighted, click the Insert button.

3. The Add Item window will appear. Click on the Menu radio button.

4. Enter Art and Design or whatever you are calling your list and choose OK.

5. You will be returned to the Menu Editor and you should see your new submenu in the Items field (set off by a >).

6. You can now select the Art and Design hotlist in the Menus field to begin adding documents (or you can select the new submenu as your Current Hotlist and then start building the list as you travel through cyberspace).

Sharing Hotlists

If you want to share one or more of your lists with other Mosaic users,

1. Close the Mosaic program and open up the mosaic.ini file.

2. Find the list you want to send to someone. Highlight the Title/URLs of these items.

3. Select Notepad's Copy command from the Edit menu.

4. You can now paste this list into a new text document that can be sent to another Mosaic user.

Note: Unfortunately there is currently no way of automatically exporting or importing hotlists in Mosaic for Windows. The person who receives your list will have to cut and paste to the Menu Editor to integrate these items. Alternately, lists can be easily converted to HTML documents with each document as a link anchor. See Chapter 4 for a primer on basic HTML coding.

Navigation in Mosaic

Obviously the reason you're in Mosaic is to go places—to explore that expanding universe of hypermedia we rattled on about in Chapter 1. The main controls for doing this are located in the toolbar and the URL box at the top of the Mosaic window. After you've entered your destination, this area tells you where you're going and gives you the options of retracing your steps or instantly returning home.

The Toolbar

The toolbar is one of the most helpful features of Mosaic. It puts many of the often-used functions of the pull-down menus onto your main Mosaic window for easy access. The toolbar includes the following buttons:

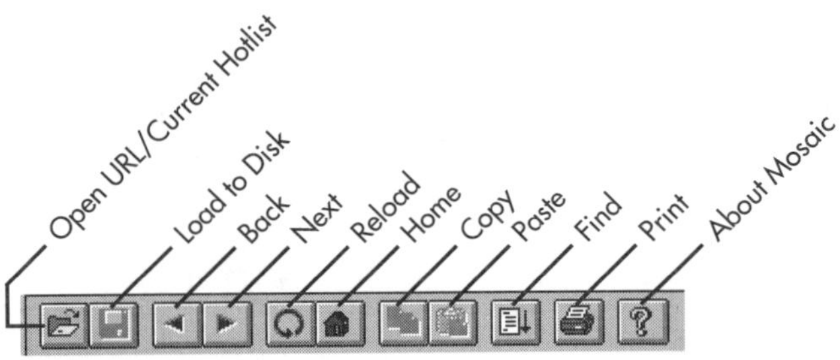

Figure 3-32: *Mosaic's toolbar.*

Open URL/Current Hotlist

This is equivalent to selecting Open URL from the File menu. The Open URL window will pop up allowing you to enter a URL or to select an existing hotlist.

Load to Disk

Allows you to save items to disk. Equivalent to selecting Load to Disk from the Options menu.

Back

The Back button (the arrow pointing to the left) takes you back through all the documents you've accessed during your session. If there are no previous documents loaded, this button will be grayed out.

A Little Background on HTML HyperText Markup Language (HTML) is a specialized set of "tags" that tells Mosaic (and other Web browsers) how to display the text, hyperlinks, images and other multimedia elements you see on your screen. These tags are guidelines for how a browser should display the material. Some tags are required by all HTML browsers, while other tags are optional. All Web browsers are different. Some, like Mosaic, are graphical, while others are text-based. Since HTML is only a set of guidelines for displaying the documents, not everyone has to have the same capabilities to access Web information. Once the HTML document arrives at its destination, the browsing software can use whatever tags are appropriate to it and ignore the rest. For instance, Lynx, another popular Web browser, supports text only. It therefore ignores the HTML style information that's not relevant to it. Mosaic, on the other hand, presents documents in all their multimedia glory and even gives you further display options. This flexibility allows you to change the way Web documents look on your system. →

Next

The Next button (the arrow pointing to the right) takes you forward to any documents that are "ahead" in the documents that have already been loaded. This button is only available if there are forward documents available (documents that you've accessed during your session, but then moved back through in the document queue).

Reload

Causes the current Web page to be redrawn in the document view window. Some sites also use the reload command as a way of loading a series of pictures. Instead of going to several Web pages to view a succession of images, you stay on one page and hit Reload to see new images. Reload is also used when you make changes in or delete an annotation and you want the changes to take effect immediately.

Home

Clicking this icon at any time during your Mosaic session takes you back to your designated home page. If you have not changed your home page in the mosaic.ini file, clicking Home takes you back to the Web server at NCSA.

Note: Back, Next, Reload and Home are also available under the Navigate menu. They work exactly the same as their toolbar equivalents.

Copy

Copies selected text. You can copy text from any of the data entry boxes, URL boxes and from the Document Source window. At this time, you cannot copy material from Web documents. Hopefully the NCSA developers will implement this in the future (the Mac version already allows it). For now, you can use the Save As command under the File menu to save text documents to disk. A copy command is also available in the Edit menu.

For more information on how HTML works, check out the following Web documents:
The HTML Primer at http://www.ncsa.uiuc.edu/General/Internet/WWW/HTMLPrimer.html and the HTML Documentation at http://www.ucc.ie/info/net/htmldoc.html

Paste

Pastes the contents of the Clipboard into the active pop-up window. You cannot copy things into Web documents.

Find

Locates text within the currently displayed document. A window pops up asking "Find What:". A Find command is also available in the Edit menu.

Print

Prints the currently selected document. If you want the printing to be the same as what you see in Mosaic, you must have scalable versions of the fonts installed on your system. Check font selections (and change as needed) in the Choose Font section of the Options menu. A print command is also available in the File menu.

About Mosaic

Displays the About Mosaic information panel.

The URL Box

In Mosaic 2.x, you can enter URLs directly into the URL box. Press Enter and the connection to an HTTP server will be attempted. The URL box will always display the currently selected Web document. See below for more detailed information on URLs.

Figure 3-33: *The Document URL window.*

Note: The other method of entering URLs is found under the File menu as Open URL... (or Control+O).

The Mosaic Status Indicator

Figure 3-34: *The Status Indicator.*

The planet icon in the upper right-hand corner of the Main Mosaic window is called the Status Indicator (or simply the NCSA logo). When Mosaic is searching for a URL or otherwise involved in a data transfer, the Status Indicator becomes animated, with little "lights" zooming around the spinning Earth (neat, eh?).

The Status Indicator can also be used for canceling a document transfer. If, in the middle of a download, you decide that you don't want to continue, simply click on the animated Status Indicator and the transfer will be terminated.

The Status Bar Message Area

This area, directly below the document view window, displays messages about what's happening during your session when Mosaic is connecting to a site, downloading documents or having trouble with a transfer. These messages can be turned on or off in the Options menu (Show Status Bar). See Figure 3-35.

Figure 3-35: *The Status bar message area.*

History

Next to the toolbar, URL box and Status Indicator, perhaps the most important navigation feature in Mosaic is the History list (located under the Navigate menu). Unfortunately there is no icon on the toolbar and no quick key that you can use to access History. You have to go to the Navigate menu each time you want to access it.

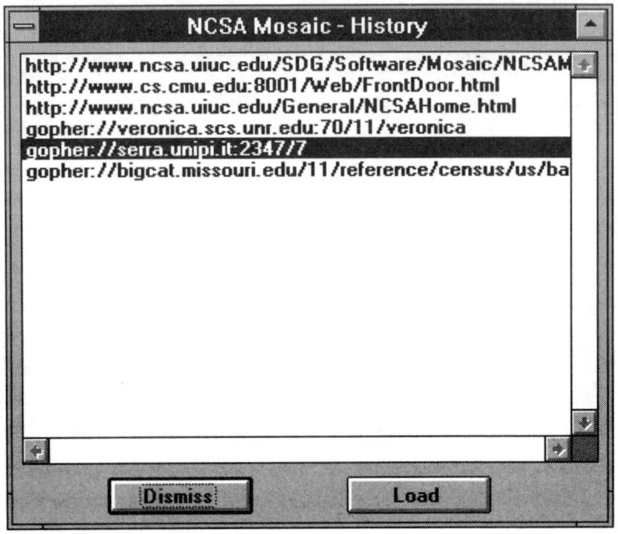

Figure 3-36: *The History window.*

Search

When you access an online index or document with lookup features, the Search box appears in the bottom of the document view window (directly above the Status bar). Search is different than the Find command (located under the Edit menu), which only looks within the current document for specified text matches. Search looks through an index of documents on your keyword(s) and then presents you with a hyperlinked list of the relevant items the search has uncovered. From this list, you can click on any of the linked documents to view them. See Figure 3-37.

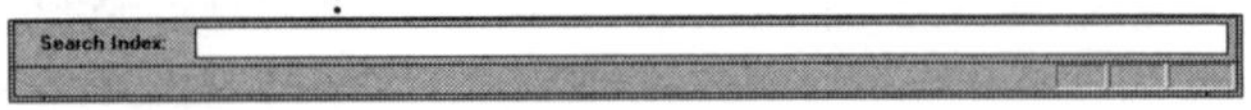

Figure 3-37: *The Search Index box.*

What Is a URL?

Uniform Resource Locator (or URL) is a system that the World Wide Web uses to standardize the addresses of various types of Internet services. Each type of service, HTTP (HTML document transfer), Gopher, FTP, USENET News, etc., has a constant type of URL address that Web browsing software can read. Although these addresses are lengthy, and look intimidating at first, they become easier to read as you get more familiar with their structure.

Anatomy of a URL

A URL usually consists of three parts: the method of access, the location of the computer where the desired files or services are available and the path to those files.

- The Access Method (or Protocol)

  This is the first part of the address, usually separated from the rest of the address by a colon and a double slash (://). This tells Mosaic what type of service it will be connecting to.

- Location of Computer Site

  The name of the computer site where the service or file is located (usually found directly after the double slash).

- File Pathname

  The specific name and location of the file being sought. This can be anything from the name of a file directory to the full path to the file itself. Sometimes a URL consists of only the first two parts with no file specified (i.e., http://www.wired.com).

Access Method	Type of Access
http	World Wide Web server file (HyperText Transport Protocol)
file	Files on your local system or on anonymous FTP server
ftp	Remote file transfers (File Transport Protocol)
gopher	Connects you to a Gopher server
news	USENET Newsgroups (reading only)

Table 3-6: *Common types of URLs.*

Reading URLs

The basic structure of a URL looks like this:

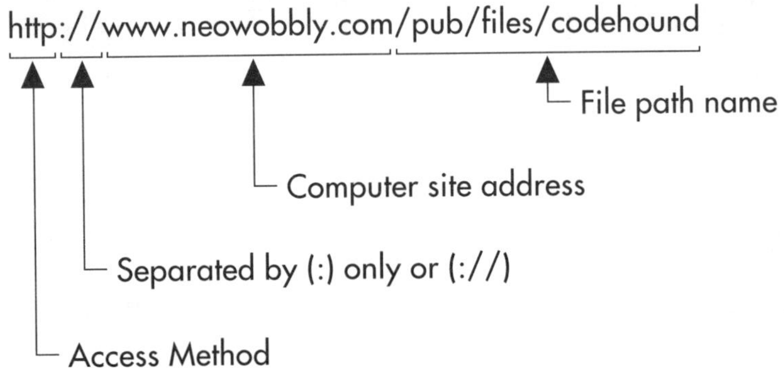

Here are some examples of URLs and what they mean:

http://www.wired.com
http://www.wired.com/Etext/2.07/features/patents.extras.html
The first http URL takes you to the home page of the WWW server at wired.com, an electronic magazine stand run by *Wired* magazine. The second URL takes you directly to an electronic text version of an article on patents that appeared in *Wired* 2.07.

gopher://well.com
gopher://gopher.well.sf.ca.us/00/Publications/authors/Sterling/fsf/buckymania
The first URL accesses the Gopher site at the WELL BBS. The second URL goes directly to an article called "Buckymania" written by Bruce Sterling. This article is located in the authors section of the Publications directory.

ftp://ftp.eff.org
ftp://ftp.eff.org/pub/EFF/about.eff
The first URL takes you to the EFF's (Electronic Frontier Foundation) FTP site. The second one accesses an introduction to the EFF located in the EFF section of the Pub directory.

news:rec.music.industrial
news:2upl68$3b9@jimbo.muppet.bt.co.uk
The URL form for accessing a USENET Newsgroup through Mosaic is different than the other forms discussed above. Here it's just news: (with no double slash) followed by the name of the newsgroup. In this example, we have accessed the industrial music group found within the rec (recreation) category of newsgroups. The second example shows the full path name to an article located in rec.music.industrial. To find out more about using Mosaic to read newsgroups (and alternative newsreaders), see Chapter 4, "Web Walking With Mosaic."

MIME Gets a Face Lift When Mosaic displays an icon indicating that a media item is available, and you ask to have it transferred, the conversation that takes place over the Web is directed by something called MIME. Multi-purpose Internet Mail Extensions (MIME) was originally developed as a method of attaching different types of files, especially multimedia files, to regular email messages transferred over the Internet. Mosaic and the World Wide Web have adopted MIME file types to specify what application should handle the transferred file. If a text/html file is received, for example, Mosaic knows to take care of that document itself. If an image/gif, image/jpeg or other MIME file type arrives, Mosaic will send that file off to the appropriate application on your hard drive.

Moving On

If you've read through this chapter, congratulations! You now know most of what you'll need to be a Web walker extraordinaire. You at least know your way around all of Mosaic's most commonly used features. These are the tools you'll need to venture deep into the Web.

In review, three features, Helper Applications, fonts and Custom Menus/Hotlists, are important to understand before you move on. Be sure you

- Have all the Helper Applications you'll need to view graphics and movies and to hear audio clips (see page 61).
- Learn enough about how fonts and styles work in Mosaic to control the look of your Web documents (see page 65).
- Know how the Custom Menus/Hotlists feature works (see page 68–74).

In Chapter 4, we'll finally move beyond the confines of the Mosaic program and into the rich fabric of the Web itself. We'll look at how to find your way around and how to access the various forms of hypermedia that are floating about. We'll also explore the many Internet services you can access with Mosaic and how you can stay abreast of the latest news and information about Mosaic and the Web.

Now that we have the basic technical aspects out of the way and we're ready to roll, let's go for a stroll through the Web to see what kind of trouble we can get ourselves into. Cyberspace beckons.

4

WEB WALKING WITH MOSAIC

All that is gold does not glitter,
All those that wander are not lost.
— *J.R.R. Tolkien*
Lord of the Rings

Jumping into cyberspace has always been an exciting experience for me. Even my first login, as frustrating as it was, gave me the Net bug. I had acquired a funky 300 baud modem and was itchin' to see what it could do. It came with no documentation and I really had no clue how to install or use it. Sticking the circuit board inside my Apple IIe, I did get it up and running—sort of. I tried logging into some local BBSes and the newly formed (now rather famous) Whole Earth 'Lectronic Link (the WELL) in Sausalito, California. It was like hearing a radio message from a ship lost at sea. There was so much line noise in among the text that I could barely make out what was going on. But I was still fascinated. I immediately got a sense that there were all these tiny ports of call in some vast electronic ocean. There were people "in" there... talking to each other...having fun...exchanging information...building something unique. After several more noisy modem sessions, I gave up in disgust. I would have to wait for a real modem. I held out for about six months, until I couldn't take it any longer. I had to get back online to see what I was missing. I went out and bought a new computer and a 2400 baud modem, dialed up the WELL and have hardly been off-line a day since. That was 1987—several lifetimes in computer years.

Mosaic is not your parents' Internet. Until recently, the language of the Internet (and its ancestors) was rather harsh and intimidating to learn. To navigate through the Net, you needed persistence and a head for second guessing how machines "think." And, on top of that, everything had to be communicated in plain text. It was far from what you would call a user-friendly environment. Information services like CompuServe, Delphi and America Online have tried to make things easier, with login software and graphic interfaces, but they are not the Internet. The quality of the information and virtual community they offer is not nearly as impressive as the Net at large. Mosaic and programs like it will change all that. They are bringing the ease of an online service to the information riches of the Internet. And, with the addition of hypermedia and an easy-to-use document creation system, they are moving far beyond the media desert of the "old" Internet and into an uncharted oasis.

Web walking feels different than other types of Internet experiences. The beehive of activity taking place there is visible regardless of how you're logged in, but a screenful of text, however brilliant, is very different from a hyperlinked web of texts with accompanying multimedia. When I log onto the UNIX-based WELL BBS, I run through a text list of conferences, and then through topics within those conferences. I come to the end of a topic, and if I want to say something, I post a response. Then I move on to the next conference down the line. It's all very list-like—from top to bottom.

On the Web, there is this feeling of being potentially everywhere at once, or at least everywhere that's hyperlinked to the site you're on and everywhere that those subsequent sites are linked to, and so on. It feels vastly interconnective in a fashion that certainly makes "web" an apt description. Being in the Web, with its graphical user interface and all of its hypermedia offerings, is an immense thrill to a Net old-timer like myself. Having been involved in hypermedia, specifically Macintosh's HyperCard, for many years, the Web is like a HyperCard stack that spans the globe. It even has pop-up QuickTime movies, graphics windows and a Home button!

But enough hyping Mosaic for a moment. Let's stroll onto the Web and I'll show you a bit of what I'm talking about.

A Web Session

The first place Mosaic takes you upon launching is the home page. Since I don't want to add to the high volume of data traffic the NCSA site (the default home page in Mosaic), I've entered my own home page URL in the mosaic.ini file. See Figure 4-1. This page lives on my hard drive and is not actually on the World Wide Web. Once my home page is loaded into Mosaic, I can go anywhere on the Web from there. The home page I've made has hyperlinks to the Web sites I frequent. Later on in this chapter, I'll show you how to create your own home page.

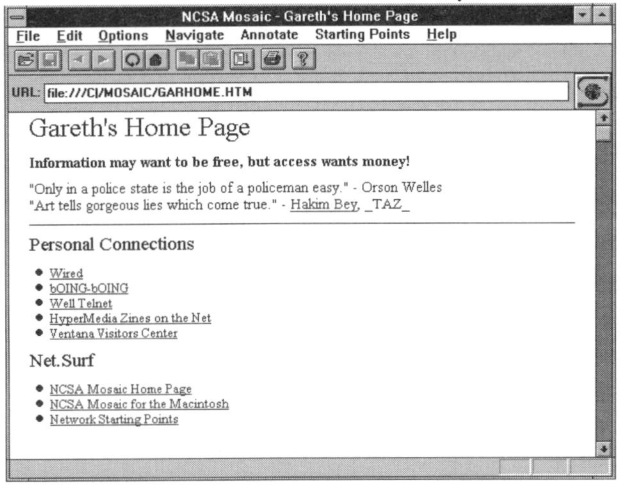

Figure 4-1: *Gareth's Home Page.*

Internet Connections List

From our home page, let's check out Scott Yanoff's Special Internet Connections List. It's a great source of links to a diverse range of Internet offerings. I press Ctrl+O to pop up the URL box and then type in the location (**http://info.cern.ch/hypertext/DataSources/Yanoff.html**). Pressing the Enter key (or the OK button) starts the connection. Once connected, Scott's List appears in the Mosaic window. It includes lots of hyperlinks to telnet addresses, gopher sites, finger sites and, of course, more Web sites.

The range of topics and interests include agriculture, ham radio, games, philosophy, aviation, careers and family issues. Since I'm in the mood for something more recreational and for sites I can show off to you, let's take a hyperlink to the Internet Mall to see if it's gotten any better since the last time I was there.

The Internet Mall

Nope. It still has a rather vacant, gloomy feeling to it, like a new real-world mall with only a couple of stores open, and all the rest curtained with signs that promise: Coming Soon! Everyone's trying to pretend that there's excitement in the air, but it's not heartfelt. The Grand Opening hasn't happened yet. The Internet Mall feels exactly like that. It's organized by floors: First Floor: Media, Second Floor: Personal Items, Third Floor: Computer Hardware and Software, Fourth Floor: Services telnet books.com. There are currently only a few items on each "floor." Not finding much of interest here, I decide to try the link to the Future Fantasy Bookstore.

http://www.kei.com/internet-mall.html

Future Fantasy Bookstore

This virtual bookshop has its real-world counterpart in Palo Alto, California. On the Web, they offer their book catalog, new book listings, back issues of their newsletters and some fantasy art. In the new book area, you can click on the name of the book and view its cover art or click on the author's name to see all the books that Future Fantasy carries by that author. Trouble is, I don't like fantasy. I came, attracted to the "Future" part of their name, but I don't see much in the way of sci-fi titles. I *do* see a link to the Science Fiction Resource Guide at Rutgers University. After goofing around for a while, looking at some full-color scans of book covers and searching on a few authors, I jump across the Web in search of the sci-fi guide.

http://www.commerce.digital.com/palo-alto/FutureFantasy/home.html

Science Fiction Resource Guide

This place turns out to be the mother lode. The Guide contains a staggering amount of information on science fiction literature, film, TV and criticism. The first thing I see is a hyperlink to "A Short History of the Internet" by my WELL buddy, sci-fi writer and cyberpundit Bruce Sterling. (Nice essay, BTW. I hope people will read it. If you do choose to read this, be sure to return to the Science Fiction Resource Guide to keep up with our tour.) Scrolling through the home page of the Guide I pass dozens of links to essays, reviews, articles, interviews, even whole books (e.g., Sterling's *Hacker Crackdown*). There are long lists of subject bibliographies, sci-fi film and TV show synopses, links to sci-fi critical journals, conventions and awards—and if that's not enough, there are links to all the other sci-fi archives in the Web!
ftp://gandalf.rutgers.edu/pub/sfl/sf-resource.guide.html

If I were on my own, I would probably spend the rest of the night scrambling along these interconnected threads, reading some of the interviews and other material available here (a FAQ for *Brazil*, my favorite movie, and a three-part FAQ on the *Alien* films). But since I'm trying to show off the Web to you tonight, I'll move on. Before I leave, I choose Add Current to Hotlist from the Navigate menu. (See "Creating Your First Hotlist" on page 68 in Chapter 3 for more information on hotlists.) I notice a link to the Best of the Net page (of which the Science Fiction Resource Guide is a worthy recipient). Let's go and see who else was so honored.

Best of the Net

A nice big blue logo welcomes you to the Best of the Net sponsored by *GNN Magazine*.

http://src.doc.ic.ac.uk/gnn/meta/internet/feat/best.html

The award winners are listed and described, with hyperlinks to each of them. The 1994 winners are (envelope please):

Figure 4-2: *GNN's Best of the Net logo.*

ArtServe

ArtServe is an art history database consisting of 2,800 images of prints, largely from the 15th century to the end of the 19th century, and 2,500 images of mainly classical architecture and architectural sculpture from around the Mediterranean. From here, you can also link to the Canberra School of Art.

http://rubens.anu.edu.au/

The Currency Converter

The Currency Converter is a script that converts currency from one denomination to another. Choose the country that interests you and view its approximate rate of exchange with other countries.

http://www.ora.com/cgi-bin/ora/currency

Edupage Newsletter

Educom is a non-profit consortium of higher education institutions seeking to transform education through information technologies. The Edupage Newsletter, published three times a week, summarizes printed news coverage of interest to all Net citizens.

http://www.educom.edu/

International Teletimes

International Teletimes is a general-interest magazine published online by sixteen-year-old Ian Wojtowicz. According to Ian, "Teletimes seeks to present informed opinion and observation drawn from the experience of living in a particular place."
http://www.wimsey.com/teletimes.root/teletimes_home_page.html

Internet Underground Music Archive

Billed as the "Net's first free hi-fi music archive." The Archive also seeks to promote obscure and unsigned bands.
http://sunsite.unc.edu/ianc/

New Zealand Information

Everything you always wanted to know about New Zealand—and then some. Geography, language, food, culture and wildlife.
http://www.cs.cmu.edu:8001/Web/People/mjw/NZ/MainPage.html

The Paleontology Server

An interactive natural history museum on the Net. Learn about phylogeny, the "Tree of Life," or examine photographs of great white sharks off the California coast.
coast.http://ucmp1.berkeley.edu/welcome.html

Science Fiction Resource Guide

"More information on science fiction than any one person can comfortably keep track of." I'll say!
ftp://gandalf.rutgers.edu/pub/sfl/sf-resource.guide.html

Taxing Times

Taxing Times is a repository of tax forms, including many electronic IRS publications.
http://www.scubed.com:8001/tax/tax.html

U.S. Census Information Server

Here you can get financial data on state and local governments as well as schools. The Census Bureau Art Gallery has a display of posters used to promote participation in the census.
http://www.census.gov/

Hypertext USENET FAQs

A hypertext database of FAQs (Frequently Asked Questions) available on the Internet.
http://www.cis.ohio-state.edu/hypertext/faq/usenet/FAQ-List.html

Xerox PARC MapViewer

MapViewer is an application that dynamically renders a map based on user input. Click on a region and MapViewer zooms in on it. You can also use a geographic name server to locate a particular location by name.
http://pubweb.parc.xerox.com/map

This looks like an exciting list of Web locations (well, I might skip the tax and census sites). First let's take a look at ArtServe. But before we do, we'll add this document (Best of the Net) to our hotlist by choosing Add Current to Hotlist from the Navigate menu. That way, we can come back and check out all of these documents at our leisure.

ArtServe

This site offers both an art and architecture collection and some art tours. You can view the databases alphabetically, with or without thumbnail images, or you can search the databases on keywords. I decide to browse through the print collection with the inline images turned off. Pressing on the image I want to see (with the right mouse button), a small thumbnail reproduction pops up. If I then want to view the entire image, I press on the thumbnail to begin downloading a larger version. When the download is complete, Mosaic opens up LView (assuming you have the LView Helper Application on your hard drive) and begins decompressing the image (see Figure 4-3). When I'm done viewing, I quit LView and return to the art database. After some more browsing and downloading, I decide to leave. But again, before I do, I'll add this site to a hotlist. I plan to come back and take a tour of the architecture section. As a graphic designer, this could prove to be a significant resource for me. Because I perceive this site as a valuable work-related resource, I add it to my "Art and Design" hotlist instead of my general hotlist (Hotlist1). From here I check out the Xerox PARC MapViewer and then call it a night. Because the MapViewer is not hyperlinked on this document, I need to return to the Best of the Net page to take the link from there. I select the History list from the Navigate menu, click on Best of the Net, and then click the Load button. From the Best of the Net page, I take the hyperlink to Xerox PARC.

Figure 4-3: *Heinrich Aldegrever (1502-1555?),* Intemperance.

Xerox PARC MapViewer

The MapViewer proves to be very easy to use. First, to find out what your map coordinates are, you have to take a hyperlink to the U.S. Geographic Name Server. By typing in the city and state in Mosaic's Search box, you find the map coordinates you want to view. The coordinates are hyperlinked. By clicking on them, you're taken back to the MapViewer and your location is plotted on the map. I typed in my hometown, Arlington, Virginia. Here's what my map looks like. See Figure 4-4.

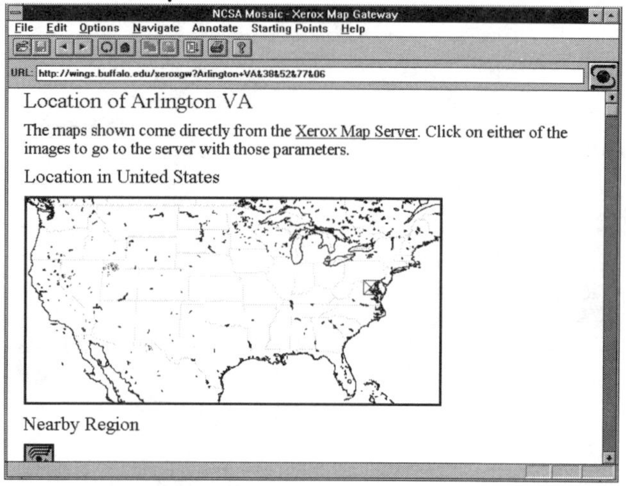

Figure 4-4: *The Xerox PARC MapViewer.*

After about two hours online, I'm bushed. I press Alt+F, X to quit Mosaic and then go to Chameleon to disconnect my PPP connection. The main thing I'm excited about from this little jaunt is the Science Fiction Resource Guide. I plan to return there as soon as I have some free time (after this book is finished!). The Best of the Net had other offerings I want to check out as well. An electronic magazine called *International Teletimes* edited by a sixteen-year-old kid seemed enticing. Toto, I don't think we're in Kansas anymore.

Now that we've had a full-blown trip through the Web and have tried some of its hypermedia offerings, let's take a closer look at how these media (hyperlinks, inline images, graphics and movies) work. In the previous chapter we looked at the features contained within the Mosaic program. In this chapter, we'll look at the contents of the Web itself and how to bring its awesome resources to your desktop using Mosaic.

HOT TIP

If you want to keep a record of your entire Web session, create a new hotlist (see "Creating Your First Hotlist" on page 68 in Chapter 3) and name it something like "Web Session [date]" or whatever is appropriate for you. Now, every time you go to a new page, select Add Current to Hotlist from the Navigate menu. This will add each new URL to your session hotlist. You'll end up with a record of all the places you visited during your session. After you quit the session, your record will be saved (unlike the regular History list).

Hypermedia in Mosaic

As we discussed in Chapter 1, hypermedia is the marriage of hypertext and multimedia (sounds, graphics, movies). While the real lifeblood of the World Wide Web is still text, its multimedia aspects are important and will become more so as the Web expands, as connections become faster and as browsers like Mosaic become more sophisticated. While onlookers may find the MPEG movies and the pop-up images of a SLIP/PPP-connected Mosaic pure novelty, the visionary knows that he or she is looking at the future. It may appear as though we're getting all excited about silent films in an age of breathtaking color cinematography, but it's the potential of the medium that's so alluring. The sense of anticipation and a spirit of cooperation is everywhere in cyberspace, with lots of people working alone or in small groups, chipping in to wire the planet for a hypermedia feed.

Right now things *are* rather crude. A SLIP/PPP-connected machine running Mosaic can be a tortoise-like media delivery system. Compressed images do well—some are downright stunning—but they take several minutes to download. Movie downloads are even slower, and the quality is often poor. Hopefully, multimedia technology will see some breakthroughs in the near future (QuickTime 2?) and Net-based hypermedia will get a much needed upgrade. Lots of sites are now using forms, user-input boxes, digital signatures, pictures with multiple hyperlinks in them and other advances in Web interactivity. Next year's Web will be a far cry from this year's Web. Or so we hope.

The main forms of media currently available in Mosaic are

- Inline Images—color and black-and-white graphics that appear as part of the Web document.
- GIF and JPEG images—color and black-and-white graphics that are transferred to your PC and opened up by an external viewing application.
- MPEG movies—moving images in the MPEG format that are transferred to your PC and played on an external movie player.
- QuickTime movies—moving images in the QuickTime format that are transferred to your PC and played on an external movie player.
- Audio—music, spoken words and sounds that are transferred to your PC and played on an external audio player.

Inline Images

Next to text, the most common element in a Web document is the inline image. These are graphics that can either be transferred with the rest of the page (if Display Inline Images has been turned on), or marked by an icon that gives the option of loading (or not loading) the image after the page has been downloaded.

Inline image icon

Hyperlinking icon

Inline images might be confusing at first because a similar icon is used to hyperlink larger graphics, sounds, movies and even other Web documents. The difference between an inline image and a piece of hyperlinked media is that inline images all load to the screen when Display Inline Images is selected. They are resident to the current document. Hyperlinked media will not load automatically. You must click on the icon to retrieve the image, movie or sound, or to go to the page hyperlinked via the inline icon. This type of hyperlinked file is also outlined in the anchor color (which is defaulted to blue).

On a directly connected Internet machine, you can choose to keep the Display Inline Images option checked. This way, you'll instantly see the whole Web page as its creator intended it, as soon as it's been transferred. On a SLIP/PPP-connected machine, having all the inlines transferred when you connect to a site can be very time-consuming, especially if you have no idea beforehand how many images are stored on the page. For this type of connection, the best procedure is to

1. Keep Display Inline Images turned off in the Options menu.

2. When you get to a site and you've read through the text, click on the inline image and hyperlink icons that interest you. Use the right button on your mouse to view the inline image and the left button to go directly to the linked file. Sometimes you will be given clues in the text as to what's behind these icons, sometimes you won't.

Really thoughtful Web page makers will put a small caption under the inline icon telling you what the item is and how large it is. Also, images are sometimes repeated on the same page (or in a series of linked pages). Since they are cached, they don't take any extra time to download.

Here are the various inline image icons encountered in Mosaic.

Inline Icon	What It Means
	Basic inline image icon with image not loaded.
	Basic inline image loaded.
	Inline image with size specified.
	Hyperlink with inline image not loaded. (If you don't want to load the inline image before taking the link, you can press the right mouse button.)
	Hyperlink with inline image loaded (by clicking on this image with the left mouse button, you will be taken to a text link or a sound, image or movie).

Table 4-1: *Inline image icons.*

Inline image icon

There are three phases to accessing something indicated by an inline image icon with an anchor color border around it (defaulted to blue). Assuming you have Display Inline Images turned off and you want to see the inline image before taking the hyperlink, you would follow these steps:

1. Using the right mouse button, click on the inline image icon with the anchor color line around it.

2. A small graphic or preview image is loaded.

Picture preview

3. If you still want to access the full file, click anywhere inside the preview image (using the left mouse button). The larger image, movie or sound will be transferred and displayed. If this icon is being used to indicate a link to another Web document, by clicking on the inline image you will be taken to the new page. In the above example, clicking on the preview image icon will bring you to a small image of Vice President Gore. Click on this image and a full-screen JPEG version of the same image will be transferred.

Note: If you don't wish to view the inline image before going to the linked item, you don't have to. Clicking on any hyperlinked inline image with the left mouse button will move you directly to the hyperlinked item.

Speaker icon

4. If the inline image icon is a link to an audio file, when you load the inline, you will usually get some type of speaker icon. Click on this icon with the left mouse button, and the audio file will be downloaded. When the transfer is complete, Mosaic opens up the audio Helper Application and immediately plays the clip.

As long as the little yellow lights and spinning planet are visible on the Status Indicator, a download is still in progress. Sometimes things will temporarily stop moving. The transfer is not complete until the lights are "turned off" on the Status Indicator and the cursor has returned from the hourglass to the pointing finger icon.

GIF & JPEG Images

While Mosaic has embedded within it the resources to present small images, larger, more complex images are best handled by one of the external viewing programs such as LView. When you click on an inline image or a text anchor that is attached to a larger graphic, the Status Indicator will light up and start spinning and the transfer will begin. Once an image has been transferred, it's stored temporarily and the external viewer assigned by Mosaic to handle that file type is launched. For GIF and JPEG images, LView is the default application (see Chapter 3 for full details on how to select other viewers). The viewer application begins to process the image and displays it as soon as it's decompressed.

After viewing the image, you can either save or manipulate the image using LView's many image tools, or you can quit and return to Mosaic. Mosaic automatically reopens the viewer each time it's needed.

QuickTime & MPEG Movies

If you encounter any movies online, you can transfer and view them if you have the appropriate players installed (see Chapter 3). It's a good idea to have both the QuickTime and MPEG players installed since Web documents will not always specify what type of format their movies are in (although MPEG is the most common). You also want to be careful to check out how big the files are before you transfer them (if any clues are given). Some movies are megabytes in size. Luckily, most Web documents do tell you the file sizes (see Figure 4-5).

Files: Size (bytes) - Date - Name (sorted)

```
 60502 - 22 Mar 09:16 - 3d-mri-brain.mpg
369069 - 22 Mar 09:16 - 3d-mri-head.mpg
740175 - 22 Mar 09:11 - BigE_Anim.mpg
339528 - 22 Mar 09:23 - DebbieHarry.mpg
730973 - 22 Mar 09:37 - IMloopy.mpg
873335 - 29 Mar 08:14 - andrew.mpg
```

Figure 4-5: *Example of how movies* should *be listed in a Web document. Some lists give no indication of movie format or size.*

MPEGPLAY is available at most of the sites listed in this book that offer Mosaic. QuickTime players are harder to find. The Movie Player is available at lister.cc.ic.ac.uk in the directory /pub/wingopher/viewers/movies/qtwplay.zip. You need the current version of QuickTime for Windows installed on your PC to use the QuickTime Player.

Figure 4-6 shows a typical movie viewer. Your mileage may vary depending on which viewers you're using. The one pictured here is MPEGPLAY (MPEG).

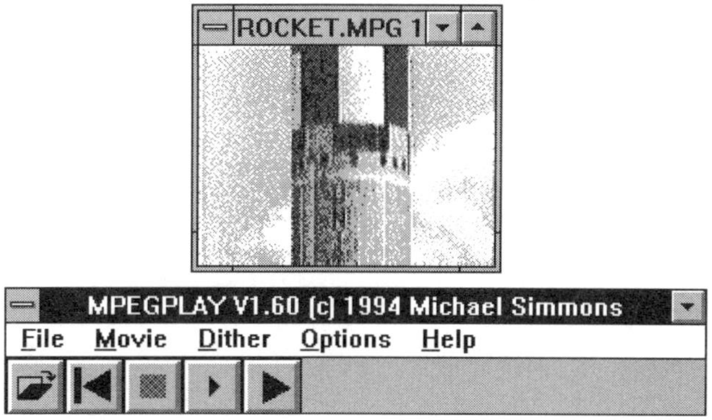

Figure 4-6: *Movie viewer.*

The way MPEG handles frame-to-frame compression is fascinating. Since most video consists of a series of objects moving in the foreground and relative static in the background, MPEG only transmits the motion of the foreground objects, rather than retransmitting both the foreground and the background over and over again. MPEG uses a form of pattern recognition to decide which pixels are part of moving objects (and therefore transmittable) and which are not.

Audio

Mosaic lets you access spoken words, music and other forms of audio. These are transferred in the same manner as images and movies. Since audio of any significant length can take up a lot of disk space (and take forever to download), look to see if the Web page tells you how big the file is before you transfer it. Some Web pages will tell you the size, others won't. Figure 4-7 shows the control window of a typical audio playback application. The application shown here is Wham. Wham can be found at **fttp://ftp.ncsa.uiuc.edu**.

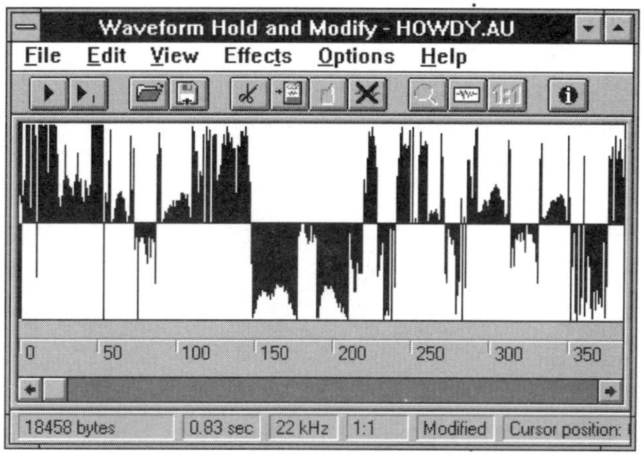

Figure 4-7: *Wham, a typical audio playback application for Windows.*

Using Mosaic as an Internet "Front End"

One of the things that distinguishes Mosaic from other Web browsers is that it's not only a hypermedia browsing tool—it can also be used to access regular Internet services such as FTP, telnet, Gopher and WAIS. You can even read

USENET Newsgroups from within Mosaic. In the following section, we'll run through each type of service and describe how you can best take advantage of it using Mosaic.

FTP

File transfer, the ability to freely move documents and programs from computers all over the Internet into your home computer, is one of the big advantages of Net connectivity. Using Gopher, Web search engines and other tools, you can find information on just about anything. If I hear about a new piece of free software, an electronic magazine or something else that's recently floated into the Net, I can usually find it and download it in a matter of minutes. File Transfer Protocol (FTP) is the main standard used on the Internet for transferring files from one computer to another. While FTPing is not difficult in any of its forms (see Chapter 2), it is especially easy with Mosaic. To access an FTP site you'll need the FTP server's URL. This address will be in the form ftp://site/filepath (if any). See Table 4-2 for more information on URL forms for Internet services. Many FTP sites are hyperlinked, so all you have to do is click on the link and you will be transported either to the site or directly to the file itself. Once you're at the site and have found the document you're looking for (usually stored in a document hierarchy not unfamiliar to Windows users), all you need to do is

1. Choose Load to Disk, either from the Options menu or from the toolbar (the Disk icon).

2. Click on the name of the file you want to FTP.

3. A typical Save As dialog box pops up asking you to name and direct the file to the appropriate directory on your hard drive. Mosaic then transfers the file. The Status Indicator lights up and spins while the transfer is in progress. The Status bar also keeps you informed as to how many bytes have been transferred.

That's all there is to it. See Table 4-3 for descriptions of many of the file types found on an FTP site and how Mosaic handles them.

Note: Clicking on the file folder or document icon within an FTP directory will do nothing (if icons are visible). These are nonfunctional internal images that are used to indicate the directory hierarchy and the various file types. You must click on the file name, not the icon, to begin the transfer.

Service Name	URL Form	Type of Service	Notes
World Wide Web	http://site[/filepath]	Hypermedia documents	Use HTTP (Hypertext Transport Protocol) for connecting to HTTP servers (Web sites).
FTP	ftp://site[/filepath]	File transfer	Used for transferring files to your computer.
Gopher	gopher://site[/filepath]	Menu-driven info. browser	Used for browsing and transferring files to your computer.
Telnet	telnet://site	Remote login	Use to connect to another machine on the Internet.
News	news:newsgroupname	Reading USENET news	You need to enter the name of your local news server in the Preferences box to access newsgroups.
Email	(not applicable)	Electronic mail	To send mail while in Mosaic, use a telnet program to log into a host that offers mail or use a mail program like Eudora.
WAIS	waisindex wais://site/database	Searchable databases	Search on keywords for text documents (mostly) that can then be transferred to your computer.
Finger	http://www.cs.indiana.edu/finger/	Get information about users	In Mosaic, you need to go through a hostname/username gateway to access the UNIX finger command.

Table 4-2: *Internet services and how to connect to them through Mosaic.*

Icon	Extension	File Type	Downloading Notes
	(none)	Directory	Cannot be downloaded. The folder icon is simply used to indicate a directory on the FTP server.
	.zip	Compressed binary	You will need the PKUNZIP utility data file to decompress. You may encounter other compression types such as .ila, .arc and .hqx, although .zip is the most common.
	.txt	Plain Text	Will be transferred to Mosaic's document view window.
	.mpg	MPEG movie format	Mosaic will transfer file and launch external MPEG player.
	.mov	QuickTime movie format	Mosaic will transfer file and launch external QuickTime player.
	.au	Audio file format	Mosaic will transfer file and launch external audio player.
	.jpg	JPEG image format	Mosaic will transfer file and launch external JPEG viewer.
	.gif	GIF image format	Mosaic will transfer file and launch external GIF viewer.
	(none)	Unknown file format	The server is unable to identify the file type.
	(none)	Telnet access	You must have a telnet program installed and in the proper filepath in your mosaic.ini file. (Gopher sites only.)
	(none)	Searchable index	Access to searchable indexes and directories. (Gopher sites only.)

Table 4-3: *Common file types found on FTP and Gopher sites using Mosaic.*

Notes:

1. External applications will only automatically "launch" if you have the appropriate Helper Applications on your hard drive and properly mapped in the mosaic.ini file. For the file types above, Mosaic has defaulted the following applications: PKUNZIP (for compressed files), MPEGPLAY (for MPEG Movies), Movie Player (for QuickTime), Wham (for audio), LView (for GIF and JPEG files). See Chapter 3 for instructions on how to locate and add Helper Applications to your mosaic.ini file.

2. The icons pictured above will not appear at every FTP and Gopher site. Some sites will not have icons at all, and you'll have to look at the extension (.mpg, .zip, .au, etc.) to figure out what type of file it is.

3. In the alpha releases of Mosaic, the FTP/Gopher icons are very finicky. Sometimes, as you navigate through the directory hierarchy, the icons will disappear and replaced by dots. Hopefully this will be fixed in future versions.

Gopher

The Internet Gophers ("go for") provide information search and retrieval on computer systems throughout the world. Connecting to a Gopher server using Mosaic works exactly the same as connecting to an FTP site. You browse through a hierarchy of directories and files until you find the file you wish to transfer. When found, you simply choose the Load to Disk option and click on its name to begin the transfer. You can access a Gopher site either by clicking on a hyperlink that's pointing to a Gopher or by typing a Gopher URL into the URL box. The form would be gopher://site/filepath (if any). Table 4-3 shows many of the file types you might encounter in Gopherspace.

Telnet

Telnet is a computer terminal protocol that lets you log onto other computers on the Internet. For instance, I use the telnet command to log onto the WELL in Sausalito, California. To do this, I log onto my UNIX account at a local Net site and then give the telnet command to "open well.com." I am instantly transported to the WELL's front door where I can log in and go about my business. In Mosaic, there is no ability to send email or to log into another computer remotely. The solution to this is to get a telnet program and point to its location in your mosaic.ini file. It will then work the same way as any Helper Application. If you come to an Internet resource that requires you to log into a remote machine to access it, the telnet address will either be typed out or hyperlinked. If typed, you'll need to enter its URL in the URL box (in the form telnet://site.domain) and choose OK. If it's hyperlinked, all you do is click on the link. If you have a telnet program installed on your machine (and linked via the mosaic.ini file), Mosaic automatically launches it and makes the connection. That's all there is to it. If you're using the Chameleon Sampler disk or Trumpet Winsock, you already have a suitable telnet program. The Trumpet Winsock applications (which include a telnet program) can be FTPed from ftp.ncsa.uiuc.edu in the directory PC/Mosaic/sockets or from ftp.utas.edu.au in the directory /pc/trumpet/winsock. Make sure you download the winapps.zip file. See Figure 4-8.

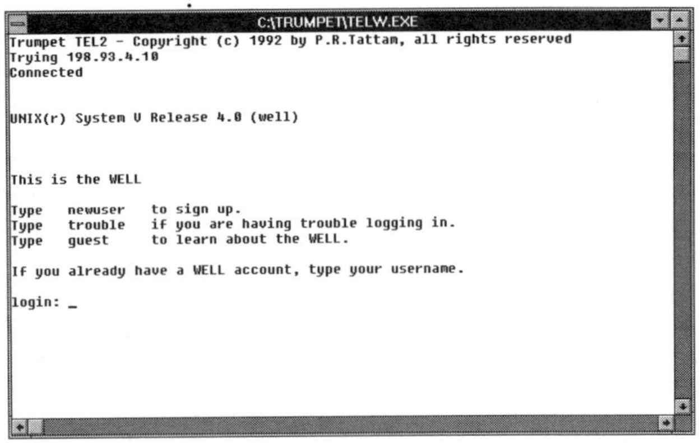

Figure 4-8: *A remote login from Mosaic using the Trumpet Winsock telnet program.*

HOT TIP

Don't forget that you can use the Windows Notepad to cut and paste URLs you find while in Mosaic or while using other Internet services. That way, by saving them electronically and not writing them down, you remove the risk of copying them incorrectly.

USENET Newsgroups

USENET Newsgroups are one of the biggest attractions on the Internet. These are discussion groups covering every conceivable subject. The discussions are often erudite, funny, feisty and bizarre. They are like global town meetings divided into special interest groups of staggering variety.

While Mosaic allows you to read these USENET groups, you can't join in on the conversations or have much control over the news feed. If, after listening in for a while, you get interested in posting messages, it's recommended that you download a freeware newsreader program and use that instead of Mosaic. That way, you'll not only be able to read the discussions, you'll be able to roll up your sleeves and dive right into them.

Reading newsgroups with Mosaic is a cinch. If you remember, in Chapter 2 we entered the address of an NNTP Server in the mosaic.ini file. This is the address of the local Internet service provider that carries USENET News (NNTP stands for Network News Transport Protocol). Mosaic accesses this local server when you want to read your groups. To access a newsgroup, you need to know its name. Many of the Internet books in the bibliography include lists of all newsgroups. Once you know the group's name, say rec.arts.tv, you need to put it in a form that Mosaic understands. This would be news:rec.arts.tv. All you do is type **news:newsgroupname** in the URL box and click OK. In a few seconds, you'll be looking at the current discussion on that topic—in this case, the latest offerings on the *other* monitor in your house.

The titles of the 20 most recent postings (called "articles") to a newsgroup appear on your screen in a hyperlinked list. To read one of

Newsgroup Readers Mosaic, for all its virtues, only gives you a peek at USENET Newsgroups. You can read groups, but you can't respond to them. If you're interested in participating in these global discussion groups, you need to use a newsreader program. There are a number of good newsreaders that are freely available over the Net. Trumpet is a popular newsreader for Windows. It is available from the following FTP sites:

FTP Site	Directory Path
sunsite.unc.edu	/pub/micro/pc-stuff/ms-windows/winsock/apps
ftp.utas.edu.au	/pc/util/trumpet/wintrump
biochemistry.bioc.cwru.edu	/pub/wintrumpet

The file you're looking for is wtwsk10a.zip.

the messages, just click on the title and the full article will be displayed. There is always a hyper-linked item at the top of the window called Earlier Articles. By clicking on this, you can access the previous 20 postings. See Figure 4-9.

WAIS

WAIS (pronounced "ways") is a text search and retrieval system similar to FTP and Gopher. An acronym for Wide-Area Information Server, WAIS gives you the ability to search databases of mostly text-based documents by using keyword queries. Similar to Gopher, you don't have to know anything about what type of database is being accessed or where it's located. WAIS deals with all this for you. Unlike Gopher, you can't browse the databases; you can only keep trying keyword combinations and hope for a match. WAIS databases cover everything from agriculture to social sciences. The easiest way to plug into the WAIS system is to go to **http:/info.cern.ch/hypertext/Products/WAIS/Sources/Overview.html**. There you'll find a master index of WAIS databases.

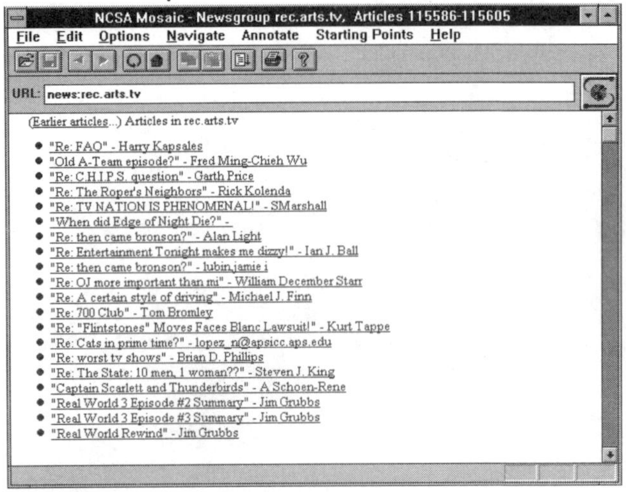

Figure 4-9: *A USENET newsgroup in Mosaic.*

Finger

Finger is a utility that lets you look up information about users on UNIX systems. Most of the time a user's Finger file consists of their login name, their real name, the last time they accessed their account and if they have any unread mail. There is also an area in the Finger file to show a "plan," which can be a bio or anything else the user wants other people to see. Many UNIX system administrators don't make the Finger files available over the Internet without the express permission of the users of their system. Some people use Finger files as a way of broadcasting information to the Net. There are Finger files with baseball scores, quotes of the day, California earthquake information and other news and trivia. These public information Finger files are traded over the Net like other cool sites, newsgroups and mailing lists. Some Net artists put ASCII-based art into their files. In Mosaic for Windows, you can access Finger files by going through a gateway that accesses Finger. The gateway address is **http://cs.indiana.edu/finger/gateway.** This site is already offered as a menu choice (Finger Gateway) under Starting Points. At the gateway site you can read more information about Finger files and the WWW gateway to them. You can also search on a Finger file from anywhere within the Web by using the URL **http://www.cs.indiana.edu/finger/hostname/username**. For instance, to view a Finger file of late-breaking NASA news, type **http://www.cs.indiana.edu/finger/space.mit.edu/nasanews**. See Figure 4-10.

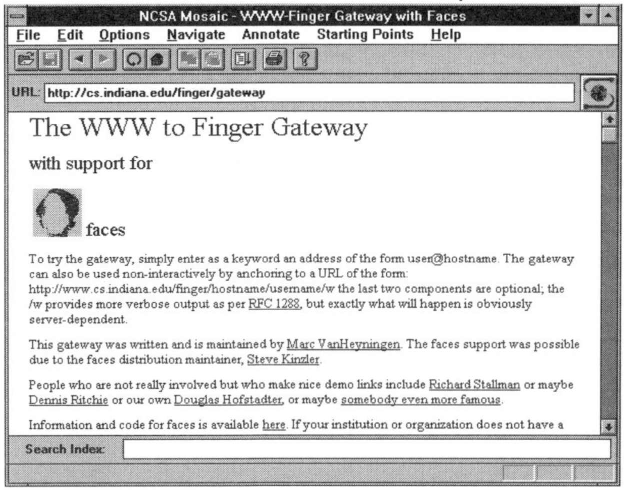

Figure 4-10: *The Finger Gateway.*

HTML ASAP: Making Your Own Web Documents

Making your own Web documents isn't rocket science—in fact, it isn't hard at all. If you can use a word processor and are familiar with fonts and style changes (bold, italic, underline), you can create HTML documents. HyperText Markup Language is simply a method for marking text in such a way that it looks and behaves the way you want it to when it's viewed in a Web browser. The marking codes may look arcane at first, but once you get the hang of them, you'll be confident in moving on to more sophisticated document construction. Let's get started by making a simple home page. All you'll need is a text editor and a little patience.

Format Containers

Browsers that read HTML (like Mosaic) use only the formatting tags you enter when formatting text. All spaces, tabs and indentations you put in the original text are ignored when your HTML document is displayed in Mosaic. So, to make things look the way you want them, you've got to use the appropriate formatting tags.

For the most part, HTML formatting tags surround (or contain) the text you want to format. For instance, if you want something to appear in boldfaced type, you need to tag the text with bold codes, like this:

<B>The Web is Wide, Wild and Wonderful</B>

The first three characters, <B>, mark the beginning of the HTML formatting. The "B" character indicates boldface. The "Less Than" (<) and "Greater Than" (>) symbols set the tags off from the actual text. The message "The Web is Wide, Wild and Wonderful" is the text that is being marked for presentation in boldface. Finally, the line ends with the code </B>. This marks the end of the area that is tagged as bold. All HTML tags end with the same </code> form.

The important thing to remember is that HTML considers most formatting codes to be "containers" that hold data to be formatted (in this case the sentence "The Web is Wide, Wild and Wonderful"). The neat thing about this concept is that you can place containers within containers. This is called "nesting" and can be used for things like applying two attributes to one object. For example:

<I><B>The Web is Wide, Wild and Wonderful</B></I>

Now our sentence "The Web is Wide, Wild and Wonderful" will appear as both bold and italic, because it is contained within bold and italic formatting containers.

Believe it or not, those are the basics. Armed with the knowledge that WWW browsers only look at formatting codes to decide how to show your text, and that these codes are containers that can be nested, you're now ready to dig deeper—constructing your own home page, complete with images and hyperlinks.

The HTML Style Tags

The foundation of any HTML document is its many formatting codes, or "tags." Table 4-4 lists the basic tags and what part of an HTML document they affect.

Begin Code	End Code	Format	Description
<TITLE>	</TITLE>	Title	What your document is called on the Web.
<H1>	</H1>	Headers	Headings differentiate between parts of your document.
<IMG SRC="">	Not applicable	Image	This causes an inline image to be displayed.
<A HREF="">	</A>	Link	A way of pointing at a different Web document, a media clip, etc.
<P>	Not applicable	Paragraph	A paragraph of text. Unlike the other formatting commands, you only have to put the <P> tag at the beginning of the paragraph.
 	Not applicable	Line break	Same as a hard return.
<B>	</B>	Bold	Shows text in boldface type.
<I>	</I>	Italic	Shows text in italic type.
<U>	</U>	Underline	Underlines a word or phrase.
<A NAME="">	</A>	Internal Link	Links to other parts of the same document.
<OL>	</OL>	Ordered (numbered) List	Causes a list of items to appear with identifying numbers next to each element.
<UL>	</UL>	Unordered (bullet) List	Causes lists to appear with bullets, asterisks or + signs next to each list item, depending on the browser.

Table 4-4: *Basic HTML formatting tags.*

Building Your Home Page

Your most basic home page would consist of a title, a header or two and some text. At this point, we won't worry about links, images and sounds. To begin,

1. Open a new document in your favorite text editor or word processing program.

2. Decide on a title for your home page. "My Home Page" is probably as good a place to start as any. Since the title of your page should appear as the first line in your HTML document, type **<TITLE>** to indicate you are about to enter the title of your page.

3. Next, type in the name of your home page and then **</TITLE>** to indicate the end of the title. Your document should look like this:

```
<TITLE>My Home Page</TITLE>
```

4. Let's put a header at the top of the page. There are six levels of header tags in HTML, with each level down a slightly smaller typeface. Since this is your top header, and you want to make it big, you should use Header level 1.

5. Type **<H1>** to indicate the beginning of your header and then type the actual header. Something like "Welcome to My Home Page." Finally, type **</H1>** to indicate the end of the header. So far, your home page HTML document should look like this:

```
<TITLE>My Home Page</TITLE>
<H1>Welcome to My Home Page</H1>
```

6. Now, add some text or a blurb about yourself. Since this information might be several lines long, you'll want to use the paragraph HTML

Top 10 Signs Your WWW Home Page Is *Not* Cool

10. Hotlist is only lukewarm.
9. Links to your page keep using the adjective "fetid."
8. Disney wants to buy the rights to use it in Mighty Ducks III.
7. On Adam Curry's list of neat home pages.
6. WWW Worm got bored and left.
5. Condemned by the housing authority.
4. Word "cool" is in the title.
3. Nancy Kerrigan says it's the corniest page she's ever seen.
2. Geek Code replaced by Geek C++ Code.

And the number one sign your home page is not cool...

1. Access log shows tons of visits by Al Gore.

—Found on the Web

tag so that it formats correctly. Type a **<P>** tag, hit enter to get to the next line and type some stuff about your home page, like this:
<P>
This is my first home page. It will be my jumping off point into the rest of the Web. Hello cyberspace!

Note: Remember, Mosaic doesn't care how many blank lines you use, or how many spaces you indent your paragraph, or where you put the line breaks. Mosaic is only concerned with the way the document is tagged. So, if you do want the lines to break at a specific point, such as in a poem, you need to put a <BR> code at the end of the line where the break should occur. This is like hitting a hard return at the end of each line in a word processor. If you do this, no matter how big or small the Mosaic window is, it will go to the next line when it encounters the <BR> code.

At this point, your home page HTML document should look like this:

```
<TITLE>My Home Page</TITLE>
<H1>Welcome to My Home Page</H1>
<P>
This is my first home page. It will be my jumping off point into the rest
of the Web. Hello cyberspace!
```

You have now constructed a working home page! A little dull maybe, but it *is* an HTML document and will function quite nicely as a home page until you want to get more elaborate. Let's go look at it in Mosaic.

7. Save your document as a text file in the Mosaic folder. Call it whatever you like (e.g., "home.htm"), but make sure it ends in .htm.

Note: On the World Wide Web, HTML documents end with the extension .html. On the PC, since extensions can only be 3 characters, all HTML documents stored on your hard drive need to end in .htm to be readable on your PC.

8. Launch Mosaic and select Open Local File from the File menu. From the Open dialog box, find your text file and click the OK button. Your home page should now load and be visible within the Mosaic document view window. How does it look?

9. To make this your permanent home page, change the Home Page= line in your mosaic.ini file by typing the file path and name of your HTML document. Also make sure that Autoload Home Page is set to yes. You've done it! Now when Mosaic starts up, you'll go directly to this home page on your local hard drive rather than having to wait to connect to NCSA. If you want to go to NCSA once you're in Mosaic, you can still get there by choosing its name from the Starting Points menu.

Adding Some Pizzazz

Face it, a home page like this is pretty boring. If you've been doing any Web walking, you know that the WWW is just bursting at the seams with graphics, sounds and hyperlinks. In fact, if you came upon a home page like the one you've just constructed, you'd probably keep right on walkin'. The great thing about HTML is that adding all the media files is as easy as formatting them!

To add a link to a picture on your hard drive,

1. Find a suitable picture. If you have a scanner, you can scan something in—a picture of yourself, for instance. Or, how about a piece of computer art? It doesn't matter what it is, as long as it's in GIF format (and not too huge).

2. Put the picture in the same subdirectory as your home page and name it <name.gif>, with "name" being whatever you choose.

3. Open your home page HTML document in your text editor. To insert a link to your picture, enter a special tag that tells Mosaic where to look for the picture when it opens your home page. Type **<IMG SRC= "name.gif">**

You need to type this in the place in your document where you want the picture to appear. For example, if you want the picture to appear below the first header in your home page, you would add the line like this:

<TITLE>My Home Page</TITLE>
<H1>Welcome to my Home Page</H1>
<IMG SRC="name.gif">
<P>
This is my first home page. It will be my jumping off point into the rest of the Web. Hello cyberspace!

4. Save your HTML document (as a text file!) and open up Mosaic. Choose Open Local File from the File menu.

If you look at the Status Indicator as your home page is being opened, you'll see that the icon lights up and starts spinning. That's your multimedia home page being loaded!

If you have the Display Inline Images option checked, your picture will appear when your page does. If you have this option turned off, you'll see an inline image icon where your picture is "stored." If for some reason your image doesn't load (if it's not a GIF or you didn't type the name in correctly) you'll get an Error Accessing message.

Now that you have a picture on the page, how about adding some sounds?

1. First, record your sound with SoundBlaster or some other PC recording application and save it as an .au sound file in the same directory as your home page. Say you record a greeting—you could call it "greeting.au".

Since Mosaic won't auto-load sounds as it does images, you'll have to put in a link anchor to your sound. A link can be anything: a word, a sentence or an inline image. In this case, we'll use a word as our link.

2. Construct the link to your sound by typing the tag into the place where you want the link to appear on your home page. For example,

<A HREF=

This tag tells Mosaic you want to link to whatever comes after the = .

3. Next, type the name of your file in quotes.

<A HREF="greeting.au"

4. To make a link show up in your home page, you need to type in the description of what you are linking to. First, type **>**, the beginning of the container for the link's name. Next, type in the name of the link as you want it to appear on your home page. In this case, let's use "Click here for greeting." Your line should now look like this:

<A HREF="greeting.au">Click here for greeting

5. To end the line, type **</A>** to mark the end of your tag. Your final sound link tag looks like this:

<A HREF="greeting.au">Click here for greeting!</A>

6. Save your home page HTML document, open Mosaic and watch your home page load. You should see your new greeting link appear. Click on it to hear the audio.

Links to the Outside World

You now have a snazzy little multimedia home page! But something important is still missing. You have no way of getting onto the Web. You need to add some hyperlinks so you can easily take off from this home page to global ports of call.

The basic format of any link is the familiar URL. If you were asleep during the URL discussion in Chapter 3, you should go back there now and brush up on what a URL is and how it works.

Before you add any links to your home page, you'll want to add a new header to indicate that this is a hyperlinks section of the document.

1. Open your home page in your text editor. Go to the end of the document. Since this header is below the first header in terms of the layout priority of the document, you'll want to use a Header level 2 this time. Type something like

<H2>Links to the Outside World</H2>

2. Now you can add a few handy links. A good one is the NCSA What's New Page. By checking this page frequently, you can keep track of all the latest Web happenings and announcements.

3. To construct a link to this page, you'll use a format similar to the one we used to link sound. The sound link was to a file on your own machine. Since here you want to connect to a file (the NCSA What's New Page) on another server, a URL is needed to make the connection. Below your second header, type **<A HREF="HTTP://www.ncsa.uiuc.edu/SDG/Software/Mosaic/Docs/whats-new.html"**

This line tells Mosaic to go to the NCSA WWW server (www.ncsa.uiuc.edu), skip to the /SDG/Software/Mosaic/Docs/ directory and grab the file "whats-new.html."

4. Just like the sound file, you need to have some way of indicating on the home page that there's a link. Add a link description similar to the one for sound. Type **>What's New on the Web</A>** at the end of the URL line. The whole line should now look like this:

<A HREF="HTTP://www.ncsa.uiuc.edu/SDG/Software/Mosaic/Docs/whats-new.html">What's New on the Web</A>

When this line loads into Mosaic, you'll see "What's New on the Web" underlined.

5. How about adding another link? Sometimes you want to search for something on the Web but have no idea where to find it. Something called a Web search engine keeps an index of all the contents of the WWW and lets you search on it by keywords. When it finds a match, you get a list of those matched items, presented as hyperlinks. These search engines are like robot librarians with a collection that spans the globe. An excellent and highly recommended search engine is called the WebCrawler. To add a link to it, go to the next line in your document and type **<A HREF="HTTP://www.biotech.washington.edu/WebCrawler/WebQuery.html">WebCrawler Search</A>**

When this appears in your Mosiac document, all you'll have to do is click on the words "WebCrawler Search" and you'll be instantly transported to the WebCrawler's home at the University of Washington.

Now that you've got two links in a row, you've got a list! Well, at least *you* think it's a list. Mosaic still thinks that it's two links right next to each other. Remember, Mosaic doesn't know diddly about text formatting! To put the two links into list form for Mosaic, you have to attach HTML tags.

There are two major types of lists: numbered and unnumbered. Numbered lists have numbers appearing at the beginning of each unique list item. Unnumbered lists have a bullet in front of each item. They both work the same way, so it's up to you which one to use. Here's how to add a list-format container:

1. Go to a point just above the first item (NCSA What's New Page) and hit Enter to insert a blank line. If you want your list to be numbered, type **<OL>** for "ordered list." If you want an unnumbered list, type **<UL>**.

2. Next to each link, type **<LI>** to indicate that the link is a *list item.*

3. Close the container by going to the line right beneath the last link and typing **</OL>** if you have a numbered list and **</UL>** if you have an unnumbered list.

4. Save your document, open it up in Mosaic and gloat—you have now constructed a full-featured home page!

You can add as many links as you like by either adding them as we've outlined above, or by cutting and pasting them from other HTML documents.

Your First HTML Document

Your home page HTML document should look like this (see Figure 4-11):

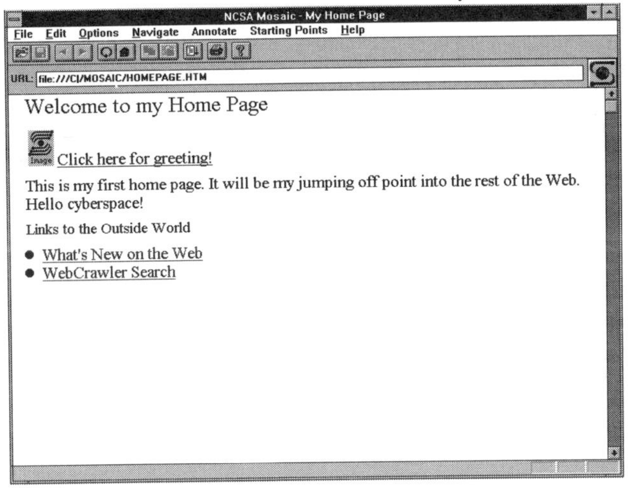

Figure 4-11: *My Home Page.*

```
<TITLE>My Home Page</TITLE>
<H1>Welcome to my Home Page</H1>
<IMG SRC="name.gif">
<A HREF="greeting.au">Click here for greeting!</A>
<P>
This is my first home page. It will be my jumping off point
into the rest of the Web. Hello cyberspace!
<H2>Links to the Outside World</H2>
<UL>
<LI><A HREF="HTTP://www.ncsa.uiuc.edu/SDG/
Software/Mosaic/Docs/whats-new.html">What's New
on the Web</A>
<LI><A HREF="HTTP://www.biotech.washington.edu/
WebCrawler/WebQuery.html">WebCrawler Search</A>
</UL>
```

Now that you've gotten your first taste of HTML document making, you may want to delve deeper into how it's done. Why not use this as an opportunity to ask your robot librarian for some advice. Go to the WebCrawler and do a search on "HTML" (or maybe more specific things like "HTML Primer" or "HTML Style Guide").

HOT TIP

A great way to learn how to create HTML documents is to look at other people's. You can mimic, copy, cut, paste and add to/change what they've done. Choose Save As... from the File menu to save a Web document to your hard drive. Open it up in a word processing program and monkey around with it to your heart's content. Remember to always save it as a text file with an .htm extension. Then, choose Open Local File from the Mosaic File menu, find the document and double-click on it. If it didn't turn out the way you planned, you can open it up again in the word processor. Make further changes, save the document and then open it again under Mosaic's File menu. The altered document will appear inside the Mosaic document view window. By tinkering and experimenting back and forth, you can learn a lot about how HTML making works.

Winning Web Page Design

With the increasing number of Net users with Web access, and thanks to the ease with which HTML documents can be created, there's starting to be a glut of really bad page designs. Terrible text layout, unnecessary use of large images and audio clips, and content of questionable merit are elements in far too many documents. As in many situations where there's a spirit of openness and an "anyone can participate" attitude, mediocrity can quickly take over. Here are a few design suggestions to keep in mind when creating Web documents.

- "KISS" is an acronym commonly used in graphic arts. It stands for "Keep it simple, stupid!" This and all basic rules of graphic design should apply to Web pages. You are publishing something that thousands of people may see. *Add* to their visual field, don't clutter it with trash. Try to keep the number of stylistic elements to a minimum and work the flow of the document so that it has as much impact as possible. An old graphic arts trick is to squint when you're looking at a page of design. By fuzzing your vision a bit, you can see the elements of a page as interacting objects rather than their specific content. Do this on your documents until the elements are balanced (or unbalanced in a pleasing way).

- Keep in mind that different types of browsers will be used to view your documents. While lots of graphics and jazzy color elements might look great on your browser, someone using a text-based browser (such as Lynx) might just see a confused mess.
- White space can be a good thing. Learn how and when to use it to your advantage. Set things off for emphasis by surrounding them with white space.
- Try to "chunk" information into logical units. Use common sense and an eye toward logical organization when you're laying out your documents. It is best to let the material unfold in levels, rather than having everything appear at once.
- Integrate your links into the material. Don't put "Click here!" off by itself with no point of reference. Your links should go where they make the most sense, ideally in context. If you do put them off by themselves, say what they are: "More information on widgets."
- Check your links! It's a nuisance to find a document that has links that don't go anywhere. Before you post your documents, make sure that everything works.

- Be literate. Again, this is as much a publishing environment as anything else. Use a spell checker and read over everything before you post it. One writer's tip: Read out loud what you've written. If it sounds good spoken, chances are it will read well on the page.
- Sign *all* of your documents. People like to know who wrote Web documents, and ideally, how to contact them. Don't just sign the "front" page of a document series. Sometimes people will come in the back or side doors to your documents (if they have a URL to a page that's not the first). If you don't label these secondary pages, no one will know whose handiwork they are.
- Give as much information as possible about the size and content of inline images and hyperlinked media. You can label inline images with a caption (57k image) or hyperlinked media with a written description: "1.2mb performance video in MPEG format." If a media item is really huge, it should have an even more emphatic message: "CAUTION: This QuickTime movie is 2.7mb in size!" (Remember, people don't read instructions. You have to shout sometimes.)
- Limit your use of inline images. Try to find small, high-impact images, and overall, use images sparingly. Think in terms of the different types of users who will be accessing your pages. Some may have fancy Silicon Graphics workstations connected to T5 lines, but others will be putting along at 14,400 baud. Try to create pages that will communicate and satisfy at all levels. It's a challenge, but it can be done.
- Don't be afraid to break any of these rules if you've got a good reason for doing so.

Staying on the Crest of the Wave

Things move quickly in cyberspace. Just when you think you have a handle on what's going on—when you think you're in the vanguard—you discover a whole new corner of the Net that you knew nothing about. Mosaic and WWW are like that. It seems as though the Web has just now caught the attention of many Net citizens. They are often shocked to learn that the Web has been around for years and that it's as large as it is. Now that you're a full-fledged Web walker, you can use the impressive resources of the Web to stay on top of its development. Listed below are many of the key documents, Web sites and USENET Newsgroups that cover the late-breaking news and announcements concerning WWW and Mosaic.

FAQs & Other Reading Material

An amazing collection of Web information packed into a single document. The *comp.info-systems.www FAQ* covers just about everything you need to know about starting out on the Web, the basics of HTML, a description of relevant terms and lots more.
comp.infosystems.www FAQ
http://sunsite.unc.edu/boutell/faq/www_faq.html

WWW Primer

The *WWW Primer* is a friendly introductory guide to the Web. Much more accessible than a lot of the FAQs and a lot better written than most "primers."
http://www.vuw.ac.nz/who/Nathan.Torkington/ideas/www-primer.html

Entering the World-Wide Web: A Guide to Cyberspace

A thick treatise by Kevin Hughes on the World Wide Web, with history, basic concepts, places to visit, a hypermedia timeline and a glossary of terms. This is a very thorough document.
http://www.eit.com/

Information Sites

Mosaic Information Site

A great starting point for seeking any type of Net/Web-related information and help. Lots of links fan out from here.
http://www.ncsa.uiuc.edu/SDG/Software/Mosaic/MetaIndex.html

WWW Information Site

The WWW Information Site graciously provides a link breakdown of WWW-related information. Users, developers, service providers and Web page authors will all find plenty of interest here. And, because it's all hyperlinked, each of the links connects to even more interesting Net points. A good place to start if you have a specific subject area you want to explore.
http://www.bsdi.com/sever/doc/wes-info

Newsgroups

news.answers

The repository for FAQ files from across the Internet. A huge body of information is accessible here. Before you ask, get the FAQs! All FAQ files that are posted to this newsgroup are archived at **ftp://rtfm.mit.edu/** or **ftp://ftp.uu.net/usenet/news.answers/**

They are also available in HTML format at **http://www.cis.ohio-state.edu/hypertext/faq/usenet/FAQ-List.html**

Tales From Hyperspace Members of the academic community have been keenly interested in hypertext since the1960s. Within the realm of progressive literature, it's seen as a writing technology ideally suited for communicating the fragmented and multifaceted nature of postmodern life. So far, most of the experiments in "hyperlit" have been done by individual authors, in HyperCard or other hypertext programs, and distributed on disk as electronic books. John Schull and Charles Deemer have a different idea. They want to grow the world's first collaborative Web novel. Called *Stories from Downtown Anywhere*, this hypertext work will incorporate many voices and many levels of talent. Anyone on the Net is free to submit work for consideration by the book's editors. Interlocking smaller stories are hyperlinked to create a larger fictional universe. If you read a story thread and see something you want to develop, a character, a physical space or anything else that strikes your fancy, you email your suggestions to the project's editors for approval. Once your contributions have been accepted, they are hyperlinked into the story. The novel is also →

comp.infosystems.announce

This newsgroup for the announcement of new information systems has also become the de facto place to announce new Web pages and sites. The University of Rochester has created a Web document announcing all the new pages announcements posted to this group. You can access the Rochester document at **http://www.cs.rochester.edu/users/grads/ferguson/announce/**

It's a good idea to add this address to one of your hotlists.

interactive, with at least two choices in narrative direction available within each story fragment.

The URL for the project is http://www.awa.com/stories/

From here, you can link to all the existing parts of the story (so far there are only a few) or find out information on how to contribute your own tales.

comp.infosystems.www.users

For discussions of browsing software, new user questions and general news, information and assistance.

comp.infosystems.www.providers

If you're interesting in setting up and administering a WWW server, this is the place to find out more about it.

comp.infosystems.www.misc

This group is set up to discuss everything not covered in the other WWW newsgroups. The future of the Web, protocols and standards have been recent topics of discussion.

comp.infosystems.www (defunct)

comp.infosystems.www was the original group created for discussing WWW. It has now been subdivided into the groups listed above. Many sites that carry USENET News still include it, but it will soon dissolve in favor of the other comp.infosytems.www.* groups.

alt.winsock comp.protocols.tcp-ip.ibmpc

These groups carry discussions of Winsock specifications and Winsock-compliant applications. Also check out newsgroups in the comp.os.ms-windows.networking hierarchy and the trumpet hierarchy of groups.

alt.hypertext

Discussions of hypertext, both in and out of the World Wide Web. People often announce their Web hypertext projects here. The FAQ file for this newsgroup can be found at **gopher://ftp.cs.berkeley.edu**.

alt.etext

Discussions on all forms of electronic texts. Not strictly related to hypertext or the WWW, but often includes postings on where to find electronic texts on the Web and how to set up your own e-texts in Webspace.

Other Applications to Ease Your Net.Life

The Helper Application scheme used in Mosaic is brilliant. As has been said earlier, it frees Mosaic up to do what it does best and it gives you, the user, the flexibility of choosing what types of applications and which specific applications you want Mosaic to use for media presentations and file decompression. Even the telnet applications, while not considered an "official" Helper Application, work like one within Mosaic (see section on telnet above). But, alas, Mosaic doesn't think of everything. Most importantly, it doesn't handle email or full newsgroup participation. Here are a number of excellent freeware programs that you can use to fill in the gaps left by Mosaic.

PC Eudora

Even if Mosaic does get email support in a future upgrade, chances are you'll still need an extra program to read mail. PC Eudora is one of the best email programs for Windows. It's compatible with Winsock and it handles SMTP and POP3 (Post Office Protocol, in case you were wondering). Like the Mac version, PC Eudora allows you to attach and receive files. To use this feature you'll need to get BINHEX.EXE. PC Eudora is also easy to find on the Net. You can get it directly from the source (Qualcomm) via **ftp.qualcomm.com** in /quest/windows/eudora/1.4/eudora14.exe.

Trumpet for Windows

Trumpet for Windows is a dedicated USENET Newsgroup reading program that uses a Windows point-and-click interface. By using a full-functioning newsreader, you not only get to read the news (as in Mosaic), but you can make the news as well by posting to newsgroups that interest you. Trumpet lets you set up lists of newsgroups you want to subscribe to, loading only the lists you want to view. You read the news by clicking on the names of the articles as they appear in the newsgroup window. To post a response, you simply choose the group and select the Post button. This is worlds beyond trying to negotiate USENET with a command-line interface. Trumpet for Windows can be found at many of the FTP sites mentioned in this book. WinVN is another popular Windows newsreader. It is available from **titan.ksc.nasa.gov** in the directory /pub/win3/winvn.

HGopher

There may be times when you don't want to fire up Mosaic just to look up some information. For those quick and dirty info grabs, you might want to use HGopher or another Gopher client. It's definitely no substitute for the hyperlinked, multimedia Web, but HGopher is still great for a quick burrow through the Net. HGopher was recently sold to FTP Software and the current shareware version (2.4) is no longer widely available (although you still may be able to find it at some sites). The earlier 2.3 is still around and is fully functional. Try the FTP site at **lister.cc.ic.ac.uk** in the directory /pub/wingopher.

WS_FTP

Even though you can easily access and download FTP-based files in Mosaic, you may still want to have a stand-alone FTP program on hand. If you are using the Chameleon Sampler disk, it comes with an excellent FTP client. A popular freeware program for Windows is called WS_FTP (or Winsock FTP). You can FTP it from **ftp.usma.edu** in the directory /pub/msdos/winsock.files.

Full Winsock Applications List

The above are just a few of the freeware and shareware applications that will work with Winsock. If you'd like a list of all the Winsock applications that can be FTPed, send an email message to info@lcs.com with FAQ as the Subject and nothing in the body of the message. The Winsock Application FAQ will be automatically returned to you.

> *Note: Most, if not all, of the programs listed above are available from the Ventana Visitors Center at **ftp://ftp.vmedia.com/pub/PC**.*

Moving On

Hopefully you've now had enough time online to understand how the Web works and what Mosaic has to offer. If you haven't tried all of its features, take some time to go back through this chapter, focusing especially on browsing the Best of the Net award-winning sites and trying out the various Internet services that Mosaic can access. Doing this will put both you and Mosaic through your paces and in Mosaic's case, make sure that it's properly configured and that all the Helper Applications are installed.

Chapter 5 is a directory of Web sites, covering everything from online libraries and art galleries to electronic magazines and recreation centers. This is not a exhaustive catalog, but thanks to the beauty of hypermedia, all these sites are connected to dozens more, which are connected to still more, and so on and so on. There are enough access points here to take you deep into the fabric of the Web, enough connections to keep you busy for years. So pack a lunch, lace up your power walking shoes and scamper onto the first available Web link that strikes your fancy.

5

SITE SEEING

"Would you tell me, please, which way I ought to go from here?" "That depends a good deal on where you want to get to," said the Cat.
— *Lewis Carroll*
Alice in Wonderland

One of the more amazing things about a good hypertext environment like the World Wide Web is how quickly you can worm your way through it, going from "cool" links to "hot" ones. In the Web walk we went on in Chapter 4, it only took a few links to travel from a very general document with lots of material of little interest to several Web pages full of material I wanted to read (and to hyperlink).

The resources covered in this chapter are far from exhaustive. There are too many sites and this book is far too modest an effort to record even a smidgen of the documents available. But the Web sites outlined below are junctions in a complex pattern of connected threads. One can lead to hundreds. If you were to act like a Web spider and follow all the links that are attached to these pages, and all their subsequent links...well...it would be a fascinating journey to say the least.

The site listings in this chapter are divided into three sections:

- General Net Resources—a veritable university on, and about, the Internet.

- Robot Librarians—indexes, search engines, databases and robots that can act as your electronic guides through the labyrinth of the Net. Learn how to use them properly and all of cyberspace will be your oyster.
- Cool Sites to Visit—some of the best, most useful and just plain weird sites and sounds available on the Web. Divided by category.

General Net Resources

It's been said that the best guide to the Internet is the Internet itself. You can put this adage to the test by going to the Virtual University represented by the listings below. Between them, they provide every level of detail you might want on Internet history, software tools, techniques and thoughts on future Net innovations. For Net vets, checking in with these sites is a good way to keep up with the latest Net technologies.

The Guide to Network Resource Tools

A hypertext introduction to all of the major Internet networking tools (WAIS, Gopher, NetNews, X.500, Hytelnet, telnet, etc.). Covers where to find them, how to use them and where to go for more information.
http://www.earn.net/gnrt/notice.html

Internaut

The online cousin to *The Online User's Encyclopedia* (Addison-Wesley, 1994), a comprehensive guide to computer networks from TCP/IP to FidoNet, BITNET, UUCP, WWIVNet and RIME. Online resources include back issues of *Internaut*, with overview articles, how-to's and letters to the editor. Also contains information about the encyclopedia and where to get it.
http://www.zilker.net/users/internaut/index.html

Internet Resource Guides

A clearinghouse of subject-oriented resource guides available on the Internet. This Web page has links to the Gopher site at the University of Michigan Library where the guides are accessible. They are divided into sections: Humanities, Social Sciences, Sciences and Multiple Subject Coverage. You can also search the full text of the collection. A number of HTML versions of some of these guides are also available.
http://http2.sils.umich.edu/~lou/chhome.html

HOT TIP

Having a problem connecting to some of the sites listed? You may be trying to access a popular site during its peak traffic hours. Don't despair—if at first you don't connect, keep at it.

The Internet Tools List

Internet Tools

A large catalog describing the various tools that can be used on the Internet for information retrieval, computer-mediated communication and other services. A number of the tool listings are hyperlinked to FTP sites so the software being discussed can be easily downloaded.
ftp://ftp.rpi.edu/pub/communications/internet-tools.html

The Web Overview at CERN

Web documents maintained by the creators of the World Wide Web. A broad overview of the Web, organized by subject, listing Web servers by country and by type of services offered.
http://info.cern.ch/hypertext/WWW/LineMode/Defaults/default.html

Robot Librarians

You're in a hurry, you need information on the Shoemaker-Levy 9 comet for a paper that's due tomorrow. Or you want to know about all the Web sites that cover film and video. Whatever resources you may be tracking through the vast halls of the world's virtual libraries, you could always use a librarian to help you. The sites listed in this section are either "self-service" information sources or they come with automated information "librarians" that will tirelessly race through the Web to find the resources you're after.

Babel Computer Terms

A glossary of computer-oriented abbreviations and acronyms. It's a shame that there are no definitions included; some of these abbreviations are quite obscure. Just knowing that POPF stands for Pop Flags isn't enough. What on earth are Pop Flags? It's still a source of worthwhile clues to the many obscure references found in computer and telecom documents and discussions.
ftp://ftp.temple.edu/pub/info/help-net

Britannica Online

The *Encyclopedia Britannica*'s online test site. Still in the beta test phase, but there are articles you can browse. Lets you search on keywords. Supports both form and list searches. This will be a paid subscription service when it's up and running.
http://www.eb.com/

CERN WWW Virtual Library

This library is the granddaddy of all Web hyperlink pages, having its humble origins in the days when the Web was text-only. The Virtual Library's "by subject" approach to Web indexing is a helpful way to begin your Web travels.

http://info.cern.ch/hypertext/DataSources/bySubject/Overview.html

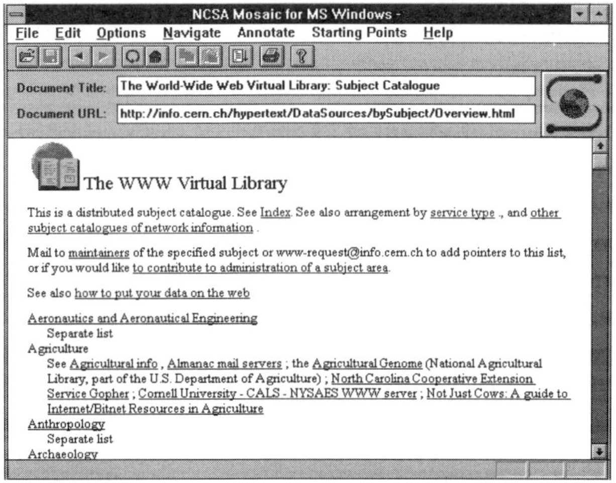

Figure 5-1: *The World-Wide Web Virtual Library.*

Dictionaries

While it might seem odd that a site in Germany is the main link point to a bunch of English dictionaries, this service is undeniably useful. Here, you can gain access to a number of literary, grammatical and lexigraphical reference books. Includes *American English*, *Webster's*, *Roget's Thesaurus*, *The Oxford Dictionary of Familiar Quotations* and an online computer dictionary. Plus many more.

http://math-www.uni-paderborn.de/HTML/Dictionaries.html

Gopher Jewels

Gopher Jewels is a moderated list service of interesting finds from Gopher sites. It covers dozens of categories on everything from agriculture and forestry to fun to library sciences. The interface is attractive and easy to use.

http://galaxy.einet.net/GJ/index.html

Index to Multimedia Sources

If graphics are what you crave, if plain text doesn't cut it for you or if you just want some nifty stuff to impress that friend who's looking over your shoulder, than the Index to Multimedia Sources is the place to go. It doesn't include a link anchor to *every* multimedia resource, but it comes close. Here you can find links to media archives, multimedia software, conference announcements, media-related companies and much more.

http://cui_www.unige.ch/OSG/MultimediaInfo

FAQ List

The FAQ List is a major repository of Net wisdom, alphabetized by subject. Perhaps the most info-dense node in cyberspace, the FAQ List lets you browse Frequently Asked Question files by pointing and clicking. From information on the Power PC to tasteless jokes and creative cooking. You can sound like an expert in no time; just read the FAQs.

http://www.cis.ohio-state.edu/hypertext/faq/usenet/FAQ-List.html

Nexor List of Web Robots

This Web Robots page links you to most of the better "robots," programs that automatically hunt the Web and index the results of their searches. Having a Web robot is like having your own data-sniffing hound dog!

http://web.nexor.co.uk/mak/doc/robots/active.html

Internet Connections List

Scott Yanoff's Special Internet Connections List is a popular Web starting point because of the wide variety of Web sites and Internet services it offers. If you want to get a better idea of the wealth of information that's "out there," try making this list your home page for a while.

http://info.cern.ch/hypertext/DataSources/Yanoff.html

SUSI Search Engine

SUSI is undoubtedly the best spider in the Web. SUSI stands for "Simple Unified Search Interface," and that's exactly what it is. Using fill-in-the-blank boxes, buttons and pull-down menus, SUSI lets you search about 40 of the Web's best information indexes. Chances are, if you can't find it here, you won't find it anywhere.

http://web.nexor.co.uk/susi/susi.html

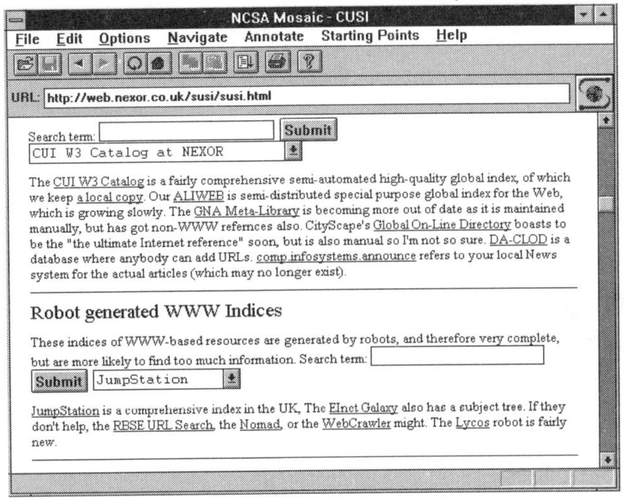

Figure 5-2: *SUSI's search engine.*

The WebCrawler

The WebCrawler serves three functions: (1) it builds indexes for documents it finds on the Web, (2) it acts as a Net-wide agent, searching for documents of particular interest to the user, and (3) it's a testbed for experimenting with Web search strategies.

http://www.biotech.washington.edu/WebCrawler/WebQuery.html

The WebCrawler icon

Wiretap Online Library

The Wiretap Online Library is an impressive collection of electronic texts. Everything's here—the classics, government reports and documents, humor, FAQ collections. Since the Online Library only exists as a Gopher site, you don't have the benefits of hypertext browsing and multimedia, but when you see what's available here, you'll probably be too overwhelmed to care.

gopher://wiretap.spies.com/

Web Searching Tips

It's one thing to wander around the Web, discovering as you go, or running down a list of links that someone's given you. But what if you have something specific you're looking for, an obscure fact, a new trend, some demographic information? Here are some Web research tips that may help you:

- Know what you're looking for. Narrow down the search as closely as possible. Find out the appropriate terminology. Often, the most difficult part about finding something is figuring out what other people call it.
- Write down your best guesses of keywords and terminology before you get online. It's easy, especially in a hyperlinked environment, to get distracted. Stay on the trail of what you came for.
- Be organized! Keep track of were you've been so that you don't end up covering the same ground. Keep a log of all the sites you visit and what they contain.
- Take notes as you go, using Windows Notepad or a resized (small) word processing window. You can cut and paste relevant material from the documents you're searching. Don't forget to match material you cut and paste with the document's URL in case you need to come back for more. Sometimes you get more useful information than you think you did. Going through your session notes, you may often find an excerpt you originally missed and you'll want to return to that document.

HOT TIP

Don't forget, you can use the Windows Notepad to cut and paste URLs you find while in Mosaic or while using other Internet services. That way, by saving them electronically and not writing them down, you remove the risk of copying them incorrectly.

- Don't put all your eggs in one basket. Often different Web search engines use different methods for organizing their indexes. Some are generated automatically, so they can include just about every Web page in existence. This is great, but you may spend a ridiculous amount of time sorting through a lot of useless information. On the other hand, some Web searching indexes are very specialized and won't ever have anything about the subject you're searching for. Diversify! Try to use a combination of techniques.
- Don't be lazy and just rely on webbed information. Sometimes it helps to use other Net resources. There's a lot of information out there on Gopher, WAIS, Archie and other searchable systems. If you're stuck in your Web searches, break out HGopher and start looking elsewhere.
- Don't be afraid to ask. Sometimes, other people are the best Internet search engines. Many people have been places you haven't; someone may have already surfed that elusive corner of the Net that has what you're looking for.
- USENET is also a great resource. Read newsgroups like comp.infosystems.www and other groups that serve people with similar interests. A quick question on a newsgroup can reach thousands of people in minutes. Sometimes, you'll receive an answer within hours.

- Don't forget the phone book (and other more conventional methods). Often, the information you're looking for doesn't require a global data search as much as it does a call to your local library, TV station or government agency. The resources of the Net and the Web shouldn't end up being a crutch.
- Keep an open mind. Just because a source at first might not seem like it's going to be useful, learn to trust your instincts and break off the beaten path every once in a while—you might be surprised.

HOT TIP

For additional words of wisdom gleaned from 23 professional data searchers, check out Reva Basch's *Secrets of the Super Searchers* (Eight Bit Books, 1993).

Cool Sites to Visit

Now that we've seen what the Web has to offer in the way of resource centers and online libraries, it's time to expand our horizons and look at some of the more culturally oriented offerings. From art and pop culture to games and virtual reality, the sites in this section give you a bird's eye view of some of the Web's cooler watering holes.

Art & Literature

One of the most exciting areas of the World Wide Web and hypermedia browsers like Mosaic is the possibilities they offer for making, exchanging and viewing art and literature over the Internet. A whole new type of art, called telematic art, has emerged in cyberspace. In telematic art, the Net and the Web themselves, and the forms of interactive communication they allow, become part of the art. You can learn more about telematic art, online art happenings, interactive literature and other cutting-edge forms of creativity at these sites. More traditional forms of art are well represented here, too.

ANIMA: Arts Network for Integrated Media Applications

Billed as "the creative cultural information source," ANIMA is divided into sections covering events, electronic art magazines, online art projects and the tools and technologies used in contemporary art. A "Guide to Online Galleries" reviews online art projects and spaces and provides hotlinks to them.
http://wimsey.com/anima/ANIMAhome.html

Figure 5-3: *ANIMA's logo.*

Art/Images

A huge database of graphics and movies covering art, astronomy, geography, meteorology, natural sciences and politics.
gopher://cs4sun.cs.ttu.edu/11/Art%20and%20Images

Art Links on the World Wide Web

Art galleries on the Web are scattered far and wide, but once found, they reveal an amazing amount of new and innovative art, music, video, photography and 3D renderings. This page contains links to most of the major and minor galleries on the Web.
http://amanda.physics.wisc.edu/outside.html

CMU English Server

Located at Carnegie Mellon University (one of the largest, most influential continents in the online world), the English Server is a valuable resource to anyone interested in cultural theory and postmodernism. You'll find everything here from serious cultural criticism to the goofier sides of trendy academia (check out "Panic Bauldrillard"). There's enough here to keep you jacked in for days, so if you pay for your Net connection by the hour, make sure to set a timer before you dive in.
http://english-server.hss.cmu.edu/

FineArt Forum

FineArt Forum is a monthly electronic newsletter covering art and technology. Besides the newsletter, they maintain a Gopher site, an online art gallery and a WWW resource directory.
http://www.msstate.edu/Fineart_Online

Jayhawk

This is an archive for *Jayhawk*, a sci-fi novel by Mary K. Kuhner, originally posted to the Net in 144 installments. Here each part is available separately and each includes a story background.
http://www.klab.caltech.edu/~flowers/jayhawk/

The OTIS Project

OTIS is a place for "image-makers and image-lovers to exchange ideas, collaborate and, in a loose sense of the word, meet." It is also a repository of images and information available for public perusal and participation. Exhibits of OTIS work have been held in cities around the globe.
http://sunsite.unc.edu/otis/otis.html

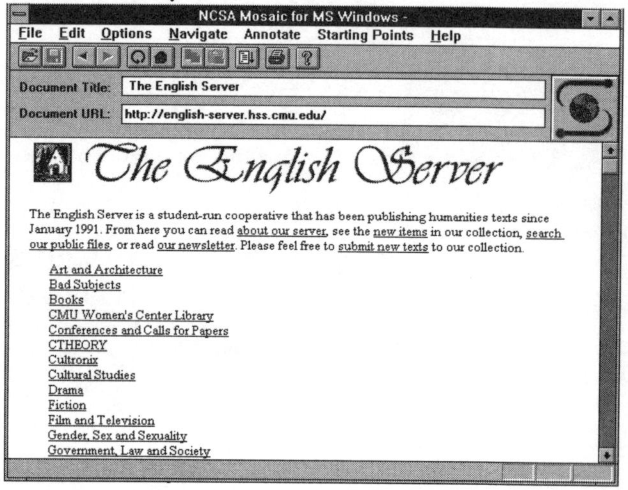

Figure 5-4: *For anyone interested in cultural theory and postmodernism, visit CMU's English Server.*

Science Fiction Resource Guide

Probably the largest collection of science fiction literature in cyberspace. Contains articles, essays, interviews, bibliographies, FAQs, sci-fi journals and information on awards and conventions. Hyperlinked to all the other major sci-fi Net nodes.
ftp://gandalf.rutgers.edu/pub/sfl/sf-resource.guide.html

Search for Images in All of Gopherspace

Don't be fooled by the fact that when you access this Gopher site you get a blank screen labeled Searchable Gopher Index. Notice that the Search box has been activated. All you do is type in key words and the Gopher searches for all images matching your request.

gopher://info.mcc.ac.uk:2347/7-tgI%20-m2000%20

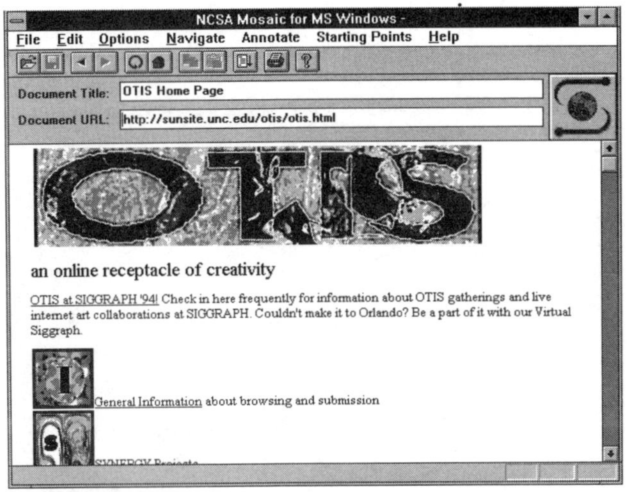

Figure 5-5: *The OTIS Home Page.*

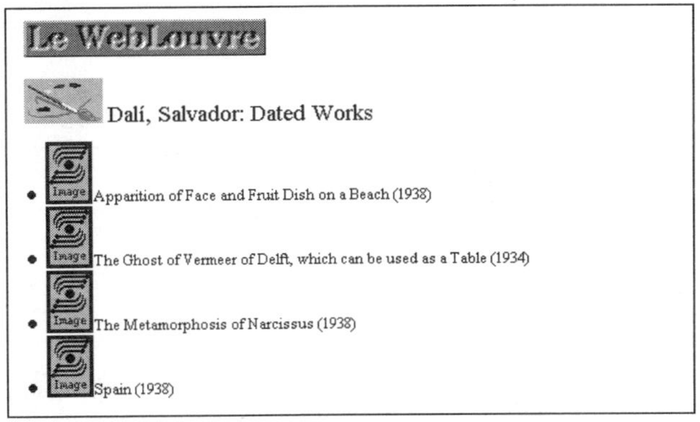

Figure 5-6: *Salvador Dali on Le WebLouvre.*

Worldwide Web Art Navigator

A collection of brief descriptions of hyperlinked sites to "get you started on your quest for art in the labyrinth of the Web."

http://www.uiah.fi/isea/navigator.html

Le WebLouvre

That's right, the world-famous French art museum is online. They are currently hosting three exhibits: a French medieval art demonstration, a collection of well-known paintings from famous artists and a tour around Paris, the Eiffel Tower and the Champs-Elysees.

http://mistral.enst.fr/~pioch/louvre/

Commerce

All eyes in cyberspace are turned toward the emerging world of Net-based commerce. Some people are excited by the prospect of doing business over the Internet, others loathe the idea, thinking it will turn it into a virtual strip mall. The bottom line is that commerce in this realm is inevitable and platforms like Mosaic are ideally suited for the online marketplace. The sites in this section represent some of the first storefronts to hang out their "Open For Business" signs.

ElNet Galaxy Homepage

This is the home page for EINet, an Internet service provider. Light on the promotional material, it is also a vital link to a number of Net resources organized by subject.
http://galaxy.einet.net/galaxy.html

The Internet Mall

A budding commercial Net enterprise with several dozen "stores" selling media items, personal items, computer wares, books and various services.
http://www.kei.com/internet-mall.html

Internet Shopping Network

Now you can "shop till you drop" at the virtual mall! On the leading edge of Net commercialization, the Internet Shopping Network offers a way to electronically shop for just about anything your heart desires. To get started, send them your credit card number and they send you an ISN password. After that, you find what you want, grab the virtual goods and the real-world equivalents are delivered to your door. I couldn't find the commemorative Star Trek: The Next Generation Borg plates, but I'm *sure* they're here somewhere.
http://shop.internet.net/

Figure 5-7: *You don't need a parking spot to shop the Internet Shopping Network.*

MarketPlace.com

Another burgeoning commercial site on the Internet. MarketPlace.com offers the Internet community a convenient and useful online shopping environment. So far they have about eight "storefronts" occupied.
http://marketplace.com

Computer Resources

If you want to stay abreast of news and information related to your computer, take a peek at these excellent resources.

PC Index

Your one-stop hyperlinked shop for PC resources on the Web. From here, you can FTP to the best and the most action-packed PC-related FTP, Gopher and Web sites, and download issues of several of the best PC e-zines. You can even connect to the American Computer Exchange to get the latest prices on used PCs and related equipment. This one should be at the top of your hotlist!
http://ici.proper.com/1/pc

What's New on comp.infosystems.announce?

The kind folks at Rochester have automated the process of keeping up on all the new Web pages as they're announced. Rather than having to spend several hours a day scanning and archiving all the new site announcements on comp.infosystems.announce, What's New scans USENET automatically and lists each new resource as soon as it hits the Net. Each listing is hyperlinked to the page announced for quick and easy Net surfing.
http://www.cs.rochester.edu/users/grads/ferguson/announce/

Ventana Visitors Center

Check out the latest news and information about Mosaic and get updates on this book. The Visitors Center is a hypertext WWW information site that supports this book, *The Windows Internet Tour Guide* and the *Internet Membership Kit*. A great source of Windows- and PC-related freeware and shareware.
http://www.vmedia.com/vvc

Cyberculture

Cyberculture is what you get when you cross digital technologies, avant-pop culture and fringe science. Inspired by the cyberpunk science fiction of writers like William Gibson and Bruce Sterling, cyberculture is concerned with the near future and how the increasing and widespread availability of high technology will affect our lives. It's a do-it-yourself mentality applied to futurism.

CyberNet

The Webmasters at CyberNet believe that the Internet has gotten far too boring, that it's lost its pioneering edge. They are dedicated to preserving "the unconventional nature of the Internet." They include a lengthy list of Web sites pushing the edges of art, science, culture and taste.
http://venus.mcs.com/~flowers/html/gcybernet.html

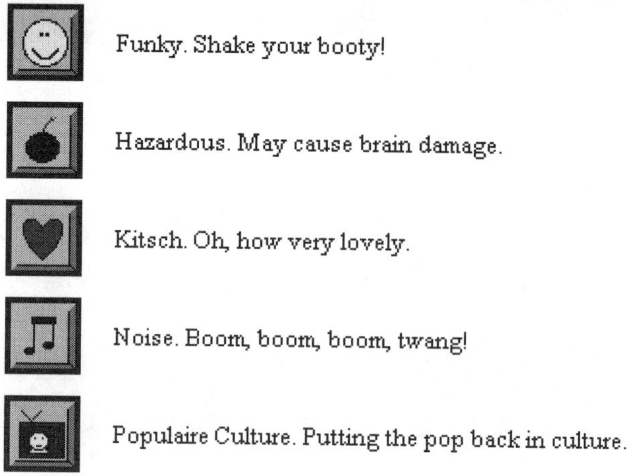

Figure 5-8: *CyberNet's hyperlink icons.*

Cyberpoet's Guide to Virtual Culture

Those who are interested in learning more about cyberculture should check out Cyberpoet's Guide to Virtual Culture. This is a popular hang-out for cybernauts. Includes essays on various aspects of cyberculture, a cyberspace lexicon and dictionary, and a huge hyperlinked database of art, pop culture, cyberculture, music, electronic magazines and more.
http://128.230.38.86/cgvc/cgvc1.htm

Electronic Cafe

The Electronic Cafe (or "ecafe" to its regulars) is a place to explore music, art, literature and virtual community. It's a place for people to meet, learn, share ideas and come together in ways that only the Net can make possible.
http://www.cyberspace.org/u/ecafe/www/index.html

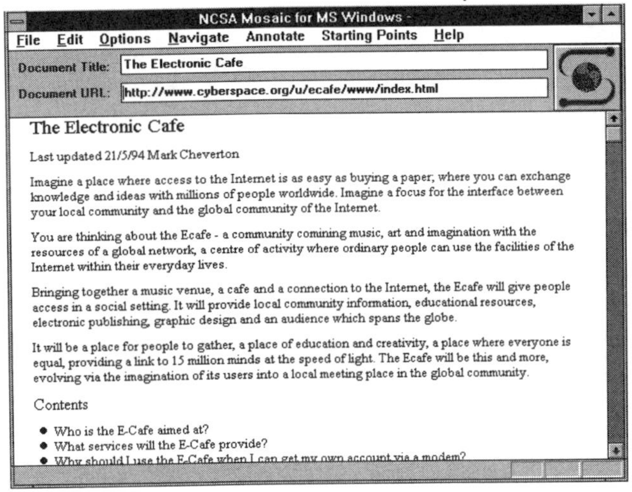

Figure 5-9: *You can get anything you want at the Electronic Cafe.*

FringeWare

FringeWare is a company and Net-based community dedicated to creating an alternative marketplace for goods and services offered by Net citizens. They publish a catalog of hard-to-find software, hardware and cybercultural curios, and two magazines: *FringeWare Review* and *Unshaved Truths*. They also maintain an Internet-wide mailing list and discussion groups on cyberculture and alternative economics.
http://io.com/commercial/fringeware/home.html

NCSA Virtual Reality Lab

The NCSA Virtual Reality Laboratory is a research facility exploring new methods of visualizing and interfacing with scientific data and simulations. The lab is located in the Beckman Institute for Advanced Science and Technology on the University of Illinois campus. The goal of the lab is to study and use improved methods of viewing and interacting with information. The VR Lab's Web site contains papers related to their research and project reports, with graphics and link anchors to FTP sites, and USENET Newsgroups devoted to virtual reality and other advanced imaging technologies.
http://www.ncsa.uiuc.edu/VR/VR/VRHomePage.html

HOT TIP

When logging onto FTP sites, it's a good idea to keep in mind what time zone you're calling. Logging into a university computer during peak school hours may leave you waiting in a long virtual line, twiddling your thumbs. Try another site where it's the middle of the night and you may have better luck. Popular information services usually have less traffic during the day and are more crowded right after school and work and on weekends. Also, whenever possible, try the sites closest to you first. Calling France or Sweden when you can get what you need from a local Internet site is wasting somebody's money, possibly your tax dollars. Be a considerate Net citizen.

neXus Home Page

neXus contains information and links that lean heavily toward the more "cyberpunk" edges of the Net. You'll find links to rave culture and music, hacking and the computer underground, industrial music and the well-known electronic compendium of cyberculture, the FutureCulture FAQ.
http://www.cis.ksu.edu/~solder/nexus.html

UK VR-SIG

This site provides access to the UK Virtual Reality Special Interest Group (UK VR-SIG) and is a major link point to VR archives and discussion groups throughout the Internet. If you're interested in virtual reality, this is the place to go to connect with the VR community online. Get information here on upcoming events, new research and development, and the latest software; view demos; and much more.
http://pipkin.lut.ac.uk/WWWdocs/LUTCHI/people/sean/vr-sig/vr-si.html

Electronic Newsstands

As mentioned in Chapter 1, a significant part of Mosaic's future will likely be in online publishing. The software and communications hardware are not yet up to par, but the neccessary innovations are just around the corner. To get a peek at the first wave of magazines that have set up newsstands in cyberspace, check out some of the following.

Figure 5-10: *Stroll through* bOING bOING*'s art gallery.*

bOING bOING

bOING bOING has brazenly dubbed itself "The World's Greatest Neurozine." In its quarterly print form it covers the wild and wacky fringes of pop and cyberculture. The new bOING bOING Online features an art gallery (mainly of comic art), articles from past issues and online exclusives. Excerpts from *bOING bOING*'s first book, *The Happy Mutant Handbook* (Putnam/Berkeley, 1995), will soon be appearing online.
http://www.zeitgeist.net/public/Boing-boing/bbw3/boing.boing.html

Fishnet Homepage

This home page is the site for an amazing one-man Internet sideshow. *Fishnet* is a weekly publication that gleans some of the best and most interesting items from the Net and stirs them together into a spicy infostew. Here you can browse back issues by date or see a list of all the subjects that *Fishnet* has covered.
http://www.cs.washington.edu/homes/pauld/fishnet

Global Network Navigator

GNN is a series of publications and information services provided by O'Reilly & Associates, the computer book publishers.

Figure 5-11: *GNN's Home Page.*

From the GNN Home Page you can access *GNN NetNews*, a weekly publication of news from the Internet, *GNN Magazine*, a quarterly with feature articles, how-to's, reviews of Net resources and an advice and commentary section, the electronic version of the *Whole Internet Catalog*, with hyperlinks to all of its resource listings, an "arcade," a travel center and The Internet Center, which includes a Help Desk for new Net citizens. You have to subscribe to GNN, but the subscription is free of charge.
http://nearnet.gnn.com/gnn/gnn.html

Hypermedia Zine List

Zines (small, do-it-yourself publications on any topic of interest) have moved onto the Net. But, like their tiny-circulation print cousins, electronic zines (or e-zines) can be hard to find. Luckily, there's a one-stop shop for electronic zine access, the Hypermedia Zine List. The list also includes links to USENET Newsgroups about zines, other zine archives and even a list of zines that are readable on the Web.
http://www.acns.nwu.edu/ezines/

Medialist

A database of email addresses for major daily newspapers, magazines, TV and radio stations, etc. Many of the entries for the newspapers and magazines include email addresses for the section and column editors (Op Ed page, Letters, Arts, Story Ideas, etc.).
ftp://ftp.std.com/customers/periodicals/Middlesex-News/medialist

Mother Jones

The Web site for *Mother Jones*, the radical expose magazine, has back issues and material related to the magazine and its mission.
http://www.mojones.com/motherjones.html

Religion and Sex: Is there a correlation?
by Wendy T

	Religion	Sex
Requires about 10% of income?	yes	yes
Many hours kneeling and sitting in uncomfortable positions?	yes	yes
Features Gregorian chants?	yes	yes
Practitioners often wear robes or other funny costumes?	yes	yes
Hundreds of books on the subject?	yes	yes

Excerpted from *Fishnet*, Vol. 3, no. 2., "A Weekly Compendium of Assorted Discoveries Found in the Crannies of the Internet."

PC Magazine Home Page

The home page for the mother of all IBM pubs—*PC Magazine*. Here, you'll find links to all sorts of neat stuff, like *PC Magazine* articles, home pages for *PC Mag* writers, back issues, and even a link to the *PC Mag* Labs, so you can get the latest low-down on your favorite hardware. Super useful and free of charge!
http://zcias3.ziff.com/%7Epcmag/

PCWeek Best News Sources & Online Mags

The *PCWeek* page is a news junkie's paradise. Nowhere else on the Net can you browse the *San Francisco Examiner* and *Chronicle*, USENET FAQs, the NASDAQ Financial Executive, *PowerPC News* and others, all from the same site. Don't be fooled though—even *PCWeek* wants to have some fun every once in a while! You can link to Adam Curry's The Vibe music server, *InterText* online fiction and other recreational sites.
ftp://www.ziff.com/~pcweek/best_news.html

PowerPC News

The latest news on the PowerPC, along with some of the most up-to-date and interesting information about the Internet and personal computing and technology in general. You can get it mailed directly to your email account, or you can wait a couple of days and read it here as a Web text.

http://power.globalnews.com/

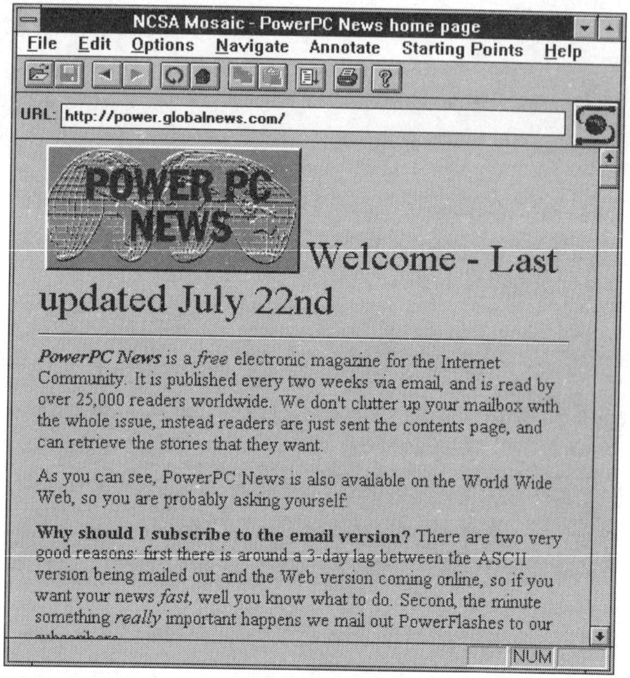

Figure 5-12: PowerPC News *home page.*

USA Today Headline News, Sports, etc...

You can telnet from Mosaic (if you have a telnet program) and read the day's issue of *USA Today*. You have to obtain an account before you're able to access the paper, but the account is free.

telnet freenet-in-a.cwru.edu
telnet freenet-in-b.cwru.edu
telnet freenet-in-c.cwru.edu
Login as: visitor

Webster's Weekly

Webster's Weekly is a weekly features magazine published exclusively on the Web. It has columns on music and movies; politics and psychology; mad rantings and humor. Published every Wednesday.

http://www.awa.com/w2/

Figure 5-13: *A sneak peek at* Webster's Weekly.

Wired

Wired is one of the most exciting new magazines to appear in years. It combines a progressive design with hard-hitting journalism from the cutting edge of digital culture and technology. Since its beginning, *Wired* has been interested in maintaining a vital presence in cyberspace. Although that involvement has so far been limited to the tools that are already available (with forums on AOL, the WELL and USENET), *Wired* is currently working on pushing the envelope of Net-based publishing. They have big plans for a new @Wired service that is currently under construction. Find out about their upcoming plans and read *Wired* back issues and special Net "Extras" at the *Wired* WWW site.
http://www.wired.com

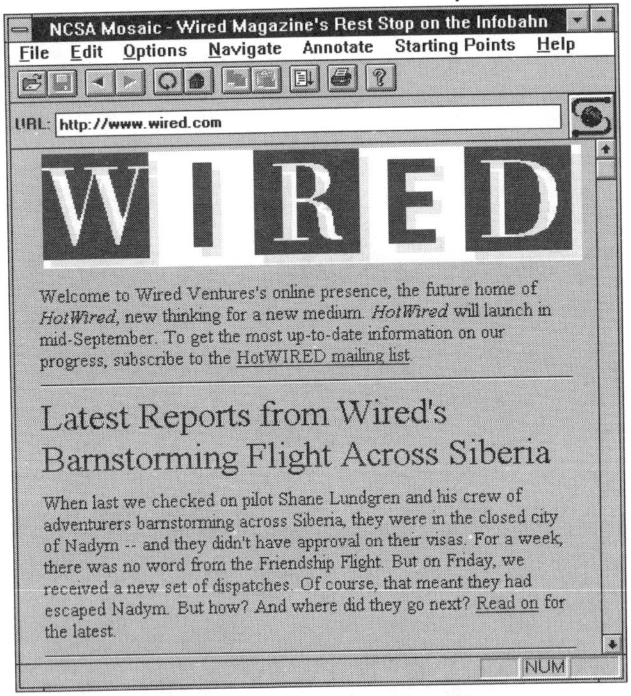

Figure 5-14: Wired *Magazine's Rest Stop on the Infobahn.*

3W

3W is a bi-monthly British magazine devoted to the Internet and the World Wide Web. Their Web site contains excerpts from the print magazine and information about past and upcoming issues.
http://www.3W.com/3W/

Fun & Games

Whether it's sports, board or role-playing games, or comedy that you're looking for, the Web has something to offer. The Net has even spawned its own brand of humor as exemplified by the Internet coffee machine and, would you believe, an Internet hot tub?

Advanced Dungeons & Dragons & Other Role-Playing Games (RPGs)

Links to game-related newsgroups, FTP sites, MUDs (role-playing games played on the Net) and other gaming Web sites. Also includes a small fantasy art gallery.
http://www.acm.uiuc.edu/duff/index.html

BU's Interactive WWW Games

The first interactive multiplayer games page on the Web. Play against a computer in a game of tic-tac-toe or pegs, try to solve the 9-puzzle—the sliding tiles game—or risk your virtual life playing Hunt The Wumpus in real time against other denizens of the Net. Things are a bit primitive at this point, but it's a harbinger of things to come.
http://www.bu.edu/Games/games.html

Doctor Fun

Doctor Fun is a single-panel cartoon by David Farley distributed every weekday over the Internet. Doctor Fun has been in production since September 1993. The cartoons are rendered in vivid colors and uploaded to the Net as 24-bit JPEG images. Farley's work has appeared in *Spy*, *Punch* and *Campus Life*, and he has done work for King Features and Recycled Paper Products.
http://sunsite.unc.edu/Dave/drfun.html

Figure 5-15: *Make your day with a cartoon from Doctor Fun.*

Games Domain

Contains links to game FAQs, FTP sites, Web pages and other Net resources related to game playing.

http://wcl-rs.bham.ac.uk/~djh/index.html

Internet Coffee Machine

It's late in the day, you've been Web walking for hours and boy are your hands tired. You want a little pick-me-up, but you don't want the nagging jitters of caffeine. How about a virtual cup o' joe? One at a safe distance—say, the United Kingdom? The Trojan Room Coffee Pot lives at the University of Cambridge in England. A special camera is trained on the pot, taking a picture of it every second. That picture is then digitized and made available to the Cambridge Web server. By typing the URL below, you can access the currently available image to see how much coffee is in the pot. This is a sophisticated upgrade on another nerdly Net gag called the Internet Coke Machine. A number of university computer sciences departments have wired their soda machines so that anyone on the Net can query them to find out how many sodas are currently available. To access the Coke machines you need to use the Finger command. If you know how to do this (see the "Finger" section in Chapter 4), try fingering drink@drink.csh.rit.edu.

http://www.cl.cam.ac.uk/coffee/coffee.html

Aliens Have Invaded Cyberspace! Bill Barker was a gallery artist living in Reno, Nevada, when in 1992, someone gave him a reprint of a bizarre article on alien invasion and abduction. He became fascinated with the subject and people's seemingly sincere tales of flying saucers and aliens among us. With tongue firmly planted in cheek, Barker began doing a series of stark black-and-white drawings, using an alien motif. He saw this as an interesting way to speak about "alienation" in all of its forms and the fears that people have about being controlled by unseen forces. The response to Barker's work, done behind the mask of a mysterious entity called the Schwa Corporation, has been phenomenal. Barker has developed a line of "alien defense products" based on his Schwa characters and themes, and these items are hot. He's developing a whole line of cheap alien objets d'art and has even been approached by a toy and a clothing company who are tickled by his strange sense of humor and his almond-headed aliens with the big not-so-friendly eyes.

The Schwa Corporation now has a headquarters on the World Wide Web. Point your URL at: http://www.scs.unr.edu/homepage/rory/schwa/schwa.html

Internet Hot Tub

If you think the Internet coffee and Coke machines are silly, how about the Internet Hot Tub! That's right, someone in Ann Arbor, Michigan, has his outdoor hot tub connected to a Sun Workstation. By sending email to the tub, you can find out how it's doing.
email: hottub@hamjudo.mi.org

Internet Hot Tub Update
Date: 94-04-01 13:22:53 est
Subj: Hottub status from hottub@hamjudo.mi.org

Paul's hot tub is nice and warm at about 101 degrees Fahrenheit. It is cold outside at about 51 degrees Fahrenheit. The ozone generator is working. The cover is closed. The access door is open. The backup battery is OK at 10.6 volts (this will still work down to 6 volts).

The Nando X Baseball Server

The Nando X Baseball Server contains baseball news, commentary, box scores, history, graphics and even videos.
http://www.nando.net/baseball/bbserv.html

Welcome to the Baseball Server

Figure 5-16: *Take me out to the virtual ballgame.*

Snapshots From the UMBC Computer Department

Probably in any other context, pictures like this would bore you to death. However, having the ability to snoop in on someone's office hundreds or even thousands of miles away *does* have its appeal. Here are up-to-the-minute snapshots of what's going on in the computer department at the University of Maryland, Baltimore. The pictures are relatively small and in GIF format, so even if you have a low-powered PC and a SLIP connection, you can still snoop. Take a peek.
http://www.cs.umbc.edu/video_snapshots/

USENET Rec.Humor Page

This page contains excerpts from the rec.humor USENET Newsgroups, it also top ten lists, tasteless jokes, song spoofs, goofy headlines and links to other humor-related sites.
http://www.cs.odu.edu/~cashman/humor.html

Kids

Kids are obviously having fun with Mosaic and WWW, too. HyperText Markup Language is easy enough that, with help from an adult, kids can create their own Web pages and attach sound and image files to them. Here are a few samples of kids showing their talents online. The Kids On Campus Internet Tour is a great way to introduce kids to the Net.

Figure 5-17: *Some signs found on the Kids On Campus site.*

SchoolHouse Gopher Server

Not pretty by WWW standards, but this Gopher site is a great resource for kids and teachers. A lot of links here.
http://crusher.bev.net:70/1/Schoolhouse/kids

Spanish Counting Books

Mr. Buckman and his students created a very cute book to teach kids how to count in Spanish. The pages were drawn by his kindergarten students using KidPics. There are audio links that let you hear the students reading the numbers out loud. You can even download an entire self-running slide show of the project.
http://davinci.vancouver.wsu.edu/buckman/SpanishBook.html

Kids On Campus Internet Tour

Every year, the Cornell Theory Center has a Kids On Campus day where kids and computers come together. The theme for the 1994 day was "Navigating the Information Superhighway," and the folks at Cornell created this huge image map of street signs to guide the kids through the various Net resources available to them. Plunk the little ones down in front of this and let 'em go to town!
http://www.tc.cornell.edu:80/Kids.on.Campus/KOC94

Miscellaneous

Here's a category for things that refused to fit into any of the other categories. Gotcha!

Best of the Net

GNN Magazine's annual awards for the overall best Web pages. Looking at these "best of" lists is very helpful when designing your own pages for Web-wide consumption.
http://src.doc.ic.ac.uk/gnn/meta/internet/ feat/best.html

Best of the Web

The Best of the Web Awards is an annual contest that gives awards to Web pages that exhibit "the quality, versatility, and power of the World Wide Web." They see their mission as two-fold:

- Promote the Web to new/potential users by showing its highlights.
- Help information providers see what they can do with HTML/HTTP.

The '94 awards were selected via a two-month open nomination period, and a two-week open voting period. The awards were first announced at the International W3 Conference in Geneva on May 26, 1994. The awards are now on permanent display at the URL listed above. Hyperlinks are provided to the 14 award winners and all the runners up, making this single site a major access point to dozens of the best sites and sounds in cyberspace.
http://wings.buffalo.edu/contest/

The Best of the Web logo

Canadian Radio

An experimental database containing sound and text files from The Canadian Broadcasting Corporation. Popular programs such as Quirks and Quarks, Basic Black and Sunday Morning can be heard online. Obviously these sound files are huge and you probably need to have a direct Internet connection to make downloading them cost effective. Ordering information is available to buy the programs on cassette tape.
http://debra.dgbt.doc.ca/cbc/cbc.html

Figure 5-18: *Get hip to the Cool Stuff in the Internet site.*

Cool Stuff in the Internet

Here's where you'll find some of the hippest links to video and multimedia on the Web. If you have a hardwired Net connection and are running X Windows, or if you have access to an X Windows system, check out the Video Browser at MIT for a glimpse of video on demand.
http://www.cs.ucdavis.edu/internet_stuff.html

Music, Film & Television

Music and moving pictures have so far not made it big in cyberspace. Powerful direct-connected machines do OK with audio and video, but for SLIP/PPP connections, at today's modem speeds, music and film can only be hinted at. The sites in this section are either pathbreaking attempts at showing what the Web can do in this area, or they're repositories of information on more traditional forms of music, film and television.

Cardiff's Movie Database Browser

A huge database of movie information, presented in an easy-to-search format. You can look up films by title, actor or even by quotes. Can't figure out what to rent at the video store tonight? Stop in here first and have a look around. Remember a famous line but can't put your finger on who said it and in what film? Search by the quotation. A film buff's dream come true.

http://www.cm.cf.ac.uk/Movies/

Internet Underground Music Archive

IUMA sports great graphics and award-winning page design (Best of the Net '94) and provides an innovative service to the Net music community. The Archive gives needed exposure to little-known bands, providing bios, commentary and reviews, and audio excerpts. Legal issues around music and music on the Internet are also covered. You need an MPEG audio player installed on your PC to be able to listen to the musical selections.

http://sunsite.unc.edu/ianc/index.html

Figure 5-19: *The Internet Underground Music Archive.*

Kaleidospace

Kaleidospace is devoted to the promotion, distribution and placement of independent artists, musicians, performers, CD-ROM authors, writers, animators and filmmakers. Artists provide samples of their work, which Kaleidospace integrates into a multimedia document. Artists pay flat rentals to showcase their work; Internet users may order from the artists online, as well as by phone, fax, email and snail mail. Kaleidospace provides placement for artists wishing to showcase their work to agents, directors, gallery owners, publishers, record labels and other industry professionals. Kaleidospace also offers Gopher and FTP services at Gopher.kspace.com and ftp.kspace.com, respectively.
http://kspace.com/

Figure 5-20: *A picture from the popular TV show "Mystery Science Theater 3000."*

Deus Ex Machina: Mystery Science Theater 3000

A meta-home page linking all of the Web-accessible documents about the popular TV show "Mystery Science Theater 3000." Animations, MST3K newsletters, pictures, sounds, show schedules, etc., are all available through this "gateway." You'll be astonished by how many sites around the Internet have MST3K-related material.
http://128.194.15.32/~dml601a/mst3k/mst3k.html

Adam Curry's The Vibe

Former MTV VJ Adam Curry has had his share of problems in cyberspace. He is currently being sued by MTV for using the Internet site name mtv.com. He's now changed his address to the one below where he maintains a number of services, one called The Vibe, which has music reviews, commentary, musician interviews, concert information, chart action and back issues of Curry's electronic gossip sheet *The Cyber-Sleaze Report*. Adam Curry's Recording Studio offers musical

selections that can be downloaded. There are also links to Web pages devoted to different rock artists.
http://metaverse.com/vibe/index.html

Adam Curry's the vibe logo

Pop Culture

Today's pop culture is drenched in technology, so it's not surprising to find cutting-edge expressions of youth culture on the Web. If you're looking to find out what today's young people are thinking and feeling, and what they're doing to express themselves, check out these two sites. The Web's Edge will connect you to many other interesting places.

Alternative X

Alternative X is an electronic publishing company focused on the '90s alternative/countercultural scene. Founded by "avant-pop" novelist, musician and essayist Mark Amerika, Alternative X's purpose is to "feature publications created by people who are actively engaged in the world of alternative art, writing, music, philosophy, electronic media and anything/everything else that might interest the emerging generation of creative thinkers and doers."
http://marketplace.com/0/alt.x/althome.html

Underworld Industries' "Web's Edge"

Underworld Industries' "Cultural Playground" is the home of Underworld Industries—a group dedicated to linking underground music, art and the Internet.
http://kzsu.stanford.edu/uwi.html

Telecommunications Policy & Information Law

Telecommunications and information law are exciting legal arenas these days. There are major commercial forces amassing on the edges of cyberspace (the cable/interactive TV industries, the phone companies, the multimedia vendors) and border skirmishes are already breaking out. While on another front, all the old rules about intellectual property, information theft and copyrights are being called into question in our digital age. If you want to watch the fur fly, or if you want to get involved in trying to steer the course of these emerging laws and policy, the sites in this section are key points of access.

Information Law Alert

Information Law Alert is the authoritative online source for news on legal disputes involving intellectual property, wireless communications and telecommunications.
gopher://marketplace.com/11/ila

Electronic Frontier Foundation

The Electronic Frontier Foundation (EFF) was founded in July 1990 to ensure that the principles embodied in the U.S. Constitution and the Bill of Rights are protected as new communications technologies emerge. EFF has been at work since then, through education, legal council and public debate, helping to shape the nation's communications policies and infrastructure. Their ultimate goal is nothing less than the creation of an electronic democracy. The EFF Gopher site contains many of their papers, articles, newsletters, action alerts and organizational materials. Other publications related to computer culture and legal issues are also stored here, as is the EFF's *Guide to the Internet*.
gopher://gopher.eff.org/00/about.eff

FCC Gopher

This is the FCC's archive of articles, releases and documents related to communications.

gopher://gopher.fcc.gov/

The Legal Domain Network

This Web site is a repository for legal information on the Internet. Here you can gain access to all the law-related USENET discussion groups such as law, alt.dear.whitehouse, alt.freedom.of.information.act, alt.politics, comp.org.eff (the Electronic Frontier Foundation), misc.int-property (intellectual property rights) and misc.legal.

http://www.kentlaw.edu/lawnet/lawnet.html

Pepper and Corazzini, L.L.P

Pepper and Corazzini, L.L.P., is a law firm specializing in communications law. Its practice covers radio, television, cable, satellite, MMDS, radio common carrier and cellular matters. Their law offices online include a very useful series of articles on issues surrounding telecom and information law.

http://www.iis.com/p-and-c

Travel

Before embarking on a trip, it's always wise to look through your maps and travel guides. You were smart enough to realize this when you bought *Mosaic Quick Tour* before trekking off into the wilderlands of the Web. The next time you manage to peel yourself away from the computer to take a real world journey, why not consult the following resources for the travel information you'll need. Be a smart traveler—don't go to Singapore with graffiti on your mind.

The Rec.Travel Library

A library of information for travelers maintained at the University of Manitoba, in Winnipeg, Manitoba, Canada. It contains approximately 15mb of travel information. Most of the information is sorted by continent and country, plus general travel info, cruise reviews, addresses and phone numbers for tourism offices worldwide, and pointers to other Internet resources.
ftp://ftp.cc.umanitoba.ca/rec-travel

Travel Information

A one-stop shop to some of the travel information found on the Net. Airline info, FAQs about tourism, specific information on countries and cities around the world, travel guides and newsletters.
http://galaxy.einet.net/GJ/travel.html

Moving On

As I write this, today's *Washington Post* has an article on the bright and profitable future of Mosaic. The piece claims that while Mosaic is a "path-breaking navigation program," it is difficult to use and so "prone to glitches" that a number of companies are having to step in and refine the program for widespread use. While it may be the case that commercial versions of Mosaic will make wonderful additions and improvements, suggesting that it needs serious work before the masses can use it is misleading. Mosaic's current popularity is due directly to the fact that it *isn't* hard to use, and certainly it's as reliable as a number of the information services I subscribe to. Hopefully, as Mosaic and the commerce around it grows, the free version will not be left behind. There's always something more exciting about using software this powerful that you didn't have to pay for (and you didn't pirate).

So there you have it my friends, Mosaic and the World Wide Web in a few easy lessons and some enjoyable datastrolls. Hopefully you now have enough knowledge and experience to be a confident and resourceful Web user. If you're still feeling unsure of yourself, or just want to expand your knowledge on the Net and the Web, I suggest you travel to some of the Web sites listed in the "General Net Resources" section above. Between those resources and the various indexes and robots available in the "Robot Librarian" section, you should have no trouble finding what you need in cyberspace. Mosaic brings an unprecedented level of access to the information and ideas found on the Net. As you become more comfortable with it, the program will move into the background and all that it offers will move forward.

APPENDIX A

MOSAIC 2.X'S IMPROVEMENTS

As this book is being written, the Internet community is excited over the public release of the much-anticipated Alpha versions of Mosaic for Windows 2.x. Early versions of this 2.x are quickly making their way across the Net. A full-blown 2.0 release should be available by the time you read this book. Here is a rundown of some of the new and improved features of Mosaic 2.x.

Interface

- Mosaic is now a 32-bit application (requiring the Win32s upgrade for Windows 3.1).
- Mosaic now supports forms. The addition of "fill-in-the-blank" boxes and forms allows Web documents to include all kinds of data input fields and other ways of making documents interactive. As more commercial entities begin using Mosaic, this will become an increasingly valuable feature.
- Error reporting is improved (see Appendix B), and more information about errors as they occur will be provided.

Navigation

- A new hotlist and user-configurable menu interface allows you to create up to 20 custom menus (in any combination of top level and pop-out menus) with up to 40 items per menu.
- A new History list fix will take you back to the last document viewed when you click the Back button. Previously, Mosaic did not update the history when users accessed cached documents.
- Domain Name Server (DNS) information is now cached.
- By using the new "Specify location of mosaic.ini file" you can tell your PC where the mosaic.ini file is stored (if you don't want to bother moving it to the \Windows directory). You specify this in your AUTOEXEC.BAT file.
- Mosaic now supports a Command Line Parameter to differentiate between a regular pathname and and a URL on your hard drive (for instance, between C:\MOSAIC\HOME.HTM and a URL such as file:///C|/MOSAIC/HOME.HTM).

Media

- It has long been a mystery as to why users couldn't type URLs into the URL box and activate links from there (rather than having to invoke the Open URL... command). Now you can!
- With the improved internal audio support in Mosaic 2.x, .au files can be played on 8-bit sound cards.
- Faster GIF decoding now loads GIF images to the document quicker.
- Transfer Bitmaps (XBMs) are now written as 1-bit bitmaps. Because of this, Mosaic can work in either 16-bit or 24-bit video mode.

- Inline images are now cached across documents. This means that if an image is in a previous document, Mosaic won't bother loading a new copy if it encounters that image again. This is very useful when paging through online publications that use the same icons and graphics over and over again.

Miscellaneous

- You can run more than one instance of Mosaic at the same time.
- Mosaic 2.x now provides firewall security support including CERN Proxy.

APPENDIX B

COMMON ERROR MESSAGES IN MOSAIC 2.X

Mosaic 2.x has improved error handling. Many of the error messages now include text instead of just error numbers. If you consistently get one or more of these errors and can't troubleshoot them yourself, contact the developers at NCSA (see the Quick-Reference Page for their email address or use the Mail to Developers item under the Help menu). Make sure you tell them

- What hardware and software you are using with Mosaic.
- What version of Mosaic, Winsock and Win32s you have installed.
- A detailed account of what you are doing when the error occurs.
- The exact wording of the error message you get.

Note: Some of these errors may originate from sources other than Mosaic. They can come from the server being accessed or from other software that is used in conjunction with Mosaic (such as your Winsock, Win32s or your TCP/IP stack). Some of these internal applications will identify themselves as the source of the error message, others won't.

-5
Mosaic has tried to download a file that doesn't exist. The file may be improperly named.

-10038
If you remain idle at an FTP site for more than 5 minutes and then attempt to change directories, you may get this message. Try reloading the FTP site.

-10048
DNS System Down, Services Not Available. The Winsock will give you this error code if the DNS server is down and cannot access the IP address of the server you're trying to connect with.

Access not available
You have tried to access an area that is not available to you.

Premature EOF
The entire document is not there and the "end of the file" has been reached unexpectedly. The file is probably damaged.

Transfer cancelled
For some reason, usually because you have clicked on the Status Indicator, Mosaic has terminated the file transfer.

No Link name specified
The link anchor you have selected has no URL specified in the HTML code. Mosaic doesn't know where to go to access the requested file. Look on the bottom of the Web document you're on, find the email address of the Webmaster and alert him or her to the problem.

Failed DNS Lookup
This is one of the most common error messages you'll encounter. This can be caused by a number of things. The Domain Name Server (a database at your Internet service provider's site that matches domain names to IP numbers) may have had a problem matching the domain, or the domain where the document you're trying to access is stored may be busy. Try again and if it still doesn't work, try reconnecting your TCP/IP stack and relaunching Mosaic. If the DNS is actually down, you should get error number -10048. Alert your network provider. If the problem persists, you can also try getting the DNS IP number(s) from a different Internet site and entering those into the DNS boxes in your TCP/IP software.

FTP Login failed
The FTP site was not able to handle your login. Try again.

Lost FTP connection
For some reason, your connection to the FTP site was terminated.

Weird error reading FTP directory
An FTP parsing error. Retry the directory (or try reloading the page and then retry the directory).

HTTP: File/directory does not exist
HyperText Transport Protocol in unable to locate the file or directory you specified. Check to make sure the URL is correct. If you continue to get the error, you may want to try moving up the hierarchy a few steps and seeing if that works. For instance, if the document you were trying to access was called http://www.college.edu/recreation/sports/golf/golf.html, you might try shortening the path to access one of the earlier documents in the queue, say: http://www.college.edu/recreation/

sports/. If you're able to gain access to one of these documents, you'll probably find link anchors to the document you were looking for.

HTTP: Error response from server

The server is having a problem. Retry the connection. If you still can't gain access, try back later.

Socket Errors

Your Windows Socket (Winsock) may give you one of the following error messages (most of them are self-explanatory):

SOCKET: Net is down
SOCKET: Net is unreachable
SOCKET: Net has been reset
SOCKET: Connection has been aborted
SOCKET: Connection has been reset
SOCKET: Connection timed out
SOCKET: Connection has been refused
SOCKET: Host name is too long
SOCKET: Host is down
SOCKET: Host is unreachable
SOCKET: Would block
SOCKET: Blocking operation in progress

QUICK-REFERENCE PAGE

Useful Email Addresses

Windows Mosaic Tech Support	mosaic-win@ncsa.uiuc.edu
Chameleon Tech Support	support@netmanage.com
Trumpet Winsock (problems, comments)	trumpet-bugs@petros.psychol .utas.edu.au
PC Eudora	eudora-info@qualcomm.com
PKWARE (PKZIP/PKUNZIP)	PKWAREInc@mixcom.com
______________________	______________________
______________________	______________________
______________________	______________________

Nifty Web Sites

Ventana Online	http://www.vmedia.com
Internaut Index (home of the TCP/IPFAQ and the Guide to TCP/IP Applications	http://www.zilker.net/users/ internaut/index.html
______________________	______________________
______________________	______________________
______________________	______________________

Useful FTP Sites

Ventana Media	ftp://ftp.vmedia.com
NCSA	ftp://ftp.ncsa.uiuc.edu
University of North Carolina	ftp://sunsite.unc.edu
University of Michigan	ftp://archive.umich.edu
Microsoft Corporation	ftp://ftp.microsoft.com

Technical Help

Built into Mosaic is a "Mail to Developers" feature. If you've put your return email address in the mosaic.ini file, then by choosing "Mail to Developers" in the Help menu, you can send technical questions or suggestions to Mosaic's makers.

You can also write:

Software Development Group
NCSA Mosaic for Windows
152 Computing Applications Bldg.
605 East Springfield Ave.
Champaign, IL 61820-5518

General comments/info: mosaic@ncsa.uiuc.edu

GLOSSARY

Anchors In Mosaic for Windows, the term anchor is synonymous with hyperlinks (non-linear links among documents).

Anchor color The color of hyperlinked items in Mosaic documents. The default color is blue. You can change the anchor color to any red, green, blue (RGB) combination.

Annotations Personal text messages that can be attached to your Web documents in Mosaic. The notes do not affect the actual document, but are available to you whenever that document is viewed. Mosaic for Windows also allows you to share annotations with a workgroup.

Archie A Net-based service that allows one to locate files that are available for downloading via FTP.

AU sounds A type of audio format used in Mosaic.

BinHex A file conversion format that converts binary files to ASCII text files.

Client A computer that has access to services over a computer network. The computer that can be accessed by a client is called a *server*. Once connected, the client can access the various services the server offers (e.g., FTP, Gopher, etc.).

Client/server architecture The client/server scheme works by having a client program (Mosaic) connect to a server program on a host computer. The client program sends requests to the server, which then takes the information request, disconnects from the client, processes the request and then reconnects to the client program to send the requested info back. This is in contrast with traditional Internet databases where you connect to them remotely (via telnet or some other form of connection), and then proceed to actually run the program from the remote site.

Cyberspace Word coined by sci-fi writer William Gibson to refer to a near-future computer network where users can mentally travel through matrices of data. The term is now often used to describe today's Internet.

Dial-up connection A connection from your computer to a host Internet-connected computer over standard phone lines. Dial-up is currently the most popular form of Net connection for the home user.

Direct connection A permanent connection between your computer system (either a single CPU or a LAN) and the Internet. This is also called a *leased line connection* because you are leasing the telephone connection from the phone company. A direct connection is in contrast to a SLIP/PPP or dial-up connection.

DNS (Domain Name Server) A server that handles mapping between host names and Internet addresses.

Document In the World Wide Web, a document refers to any file, whether containing text, media or hyperlinks, that can be transferred from an HTTP server to a client program (such as Mosaic).

Document window In Mosaic, the scrollable window where HTML documents can be viewed is commonly referred to as the *document window.*

External viewer Program used for presenting graphics, audio and movies in Mosaic. The word viewer is a bit confusing since external viewer also refers to audio applications. Helper applications, the other term used for these external programs, seems more appropriate.

E-zines Electronic zines, or small circulation publications, that are distributed over computer networks. The word "zines" comes from the print world where it is used to describe small, do-it-yourself publications.

FAQ (Frequently Asked Question) A text file on the Internet that answers commonly asked questions on a given subject. FAQs are a major source of Net knowledge and wisdom.

FTP (File Transfer Protocol) (n) A commonly used protocol for transferring files from one computer to another. (v) The act of transferring files.

GIF (Graphic Interchange Format, pronounced "jiff") A file compression format developed by CompuServe for transferring graphics files to and from online services.

Gopher A menu-driven system for searching online information resources.

Gopherspace Another term used to describe the entire Gopher network that spans the Internet.

Helper applications *See* External viewers.

Home page The document that is displayed when you first open Mosaic. Also, commonly used to refer to the first document you come to in a collection of documents on a Web site.

Hotlists Lists of frequently accessed Web location names and URLs.

HTML (HyperText Markup Language) A system for tagging the various parts of a Web document that tells the browsing software how to display the document's text, links, graphics and attached media.

HTML document Any document tagged in the HTML format. An HTML document that is accessible to the WWW is a Web document.

HTTP servers (HyperText Transport Protocol) A server computer that uses the communication protocol for Web document transfer.

Hypermedia The hypertext concept extended to include linked multiple media such as graphics, movies and audio.

Hypertext Documents that are cross-linked in such a way that the reader can explore non-linear information trails through them. (For example, clicking on a word might take you to a definition of that word or to another document related to it.)

Inline images Graphics that are contained within a Web document page. With Mosaic, these graphics can either be loaded automatically when the page is accessed or loaded manually by clicking on an inline image icon.

IP address (Internet Protocol) An IP address is a number assigned to any Internet-connected computer.

JPEG (Joint Photographic Experts Group) An image compression format used to transfer color photographs and images over computer networks.

Links Synonymous with anchors, hotlinks and hyperlinks.

MIME (Multi-purpose Internet Mail Extensions) A format originally developed for attaching sounds, images and other media files to electronic mail. MIME file types are also used in Mosaic.

Mosaic A World Wide Web multimedia browser developed at the National Center for Supercomputing Applications at the University of Illinois, Urbana-Champaign. Mosaic is made available free of charge to the Internet community. Versions are available for the Mac, Windows and X Windows.

MPEG (Moving Pictures Expert Group) MPEG is an international standard for video compression and desktop movie presentation. You need a special viewing application to run the MPEG "movies" on your computer.

NCSA The National Center for Supercomputing Applications at the University of Illinois, Urbana-Champaign. Developers of Mosaic, NCSA Telnet and a number of other freeware applications.

NEWT A custom TCP/IP protocol stack used with NetManage's Chameleon software package. NEWT is Winsock-compliant, meaning that you can use it with other TCP/IP applications that use Winsock.

PC Eudora A freeware email program (available for both Windows and Mac) that can be used over a SLIP/PPP connection.

PPP connection (Point-to-Point Protocol) A type of Internet connection where a computer can use phone lines and a modem to connect to the Internet (without having to connect to a host). PPP connections are rented from a local Internet service provider.

QuickTime A digital video standard developed by Apple Computer. QuickTime implimentations exist for both Mac and Windows. You need a special viewing application to run the QuickTime "movies" on your PC.

Server A computer that offers various services (document viewing, file transfer, etc.) to other computers (called clients).

SLIP connection (Serial Line Internet Protocol) A type of Internet connection where a computer can use phone lines and a modem to connect to the Internet (without having to connect to a host). SLIP connections are rented from a local Internet service provider.

Tags Formatting codes used in HTML documents. These tags indicate how the parts of a document will appear when displayed by browsing software (such as Mosaic).

TCP/IP (Transmission Control Protocol/Internet Protocol) A suite of protocols that the Internet uses for transmitting data.

Telnet An application that lets you log into another system using the telnet protocol.

TIFF (Tagged Image File Format) A graphic file format developed by Aldus and Microsoft. Originally intended to be used with scanners, TIFF is now used as an image transfer format on computer networks. Mosaic supports the viewing of TIFF images.

Trumpet Winsock A popular shareware TCP/IP protocol stack.

URL (Uniform Resource Locator) The addressing system used in the World Wide Web and a proposed addressing standard for the entire Internet. The URL contains information about the method of access, the server to be accessed and the path of any files to be accessed.

WAIS (Wide Area Information Service) A Net-wide system for looking up information in databases and libraries.

WAIS gateway A computer that is used to translate WAIS data so that it can be made available to an otherwise incompatible network or application. Since Mosaic cannot speak directly to WAIS, it must first go through a WAIS gateway.

Web browser Software that allows a user to access and view HTML documents. Mosaic and Cello are two examples of Web browsers.

Web document An HTML document that is browsable on the WWW.

Webmaster The person in charge of administrating a World Wide Web site.

Web node Synonymous with Web site or Web server.

Web page An HTML document that is accessible in the Web.

Webspace Another term used to describe the "space" created by the WWW.

Web spider Automated software that crawls through the links of the Web and sends back a list of all the links it's traversed. Also, Web spider (or Net spider) is sometimes used to refer to a person who really knows his or her way around the Web.

Web walking Using a Web browsing program to move through the documents available on the World Wide Web. The casual "browsing" nature of navigating the WWW has given rise to many slang terms that have to do with walking, strolling, crawling and jumping. As opposed to the more frantic metaphors found on the rest of the Internet (jacking in, data surfing, cyber run, etc.).

Winsock (Windows Sockets) A technical specification that interfaces a TCP/IP application (such as Mosaic) and the TCP/IP protocol stack (such as NEWT or Trumpet Winsock) used to connect with the Internet. Winsock provides compatibility between TCP/IP applications. On your PC, Winsock appears as a DLL (Dynamic Link Library) file. Most vendors of TCP/IP software are now using the Winsock standard.

World Wide Web The hypermedia document presentation system that can be accessed over the Internet using software called a browser. Mosaic is such a Web browser. Abbreviated WWW.

Zines *See* E-zines.

BIBLIOGRAPHY

Books

Aboba, Bernard. *The Online User's Encyclopedia*. New York, NY: Addison-Wesley, 1994.

Basch, Reva. *Secrets of the Super Searchers*. Wilton, CT: Eight Bit Books, 1993.

Bayers, Albert F. III, Peter Rutten, and Kelly Maloni. *Net Guide*. New York, NY: Random House, 1994.

Fraase, Michael. *The Windows Internet Tour Guide*. Chapel Hill, NC: Ventana Press, 1994.

Hahn, Harley, and Rick Stout. *The Internet Complete Reference*. Berkeley, CA: Osborne McGraw-Hill, 1994.

———. *The Internet Yellow Pages*. Berkeley, CA: Osborne McGraw-Hill, 1994.

Kirby, Doug, Mike Wilkins, and Ken Smith. *New Roadside America*. New York, NY: Simon & Schuster, 1992.

Krol, Ed. *The Whole Internet User's Guide and Catalog*. Second edition. Sebastopol, CA: O'Reilly & Associates, 1994.

Lambert, S., and W. Howe. *Internet Basics*. New York, NY: Random House, 1994.

McLuhan, Marshall. *Understanding Media: The Extensions of Man*. New York: McGraw-Hill, 1965.

Rheingold, Howard. *The Virtual Community: Homesteading on the Electronic Frontier*. New York, NY: Addison-Wesley, 1993.

Stephenson, Neil. *Snow Crash*. New York, NY: Bantam, 1992.

Williams, Robin. *Jargon: An Informal Dictionary of Computer Terms*. Berkeley, CA: Peachpit Press, 1993.

Periodicals

3W—The World Wide Web Newsletter, 461 West 49th St., Suite 338, New York, NY 10019. Bi-monthly.

Wired, P.O. Box 191826, San Francisco, CA 94119-9866. Monthly.

INDEX

A

B

C

D

E

F

G

H

I

J

L

M

N

O

P

Q

R

S

T

COLOPHON

This book was developed on a Macintosh Quadra 650. All pages were produced in Aldus PageMaker 5.0. Some graphics were produced or edited in Adobe Photoshop 2.5.1 and Adobe Illustrator 5.0. Chapter titles are set in Anna. Chapter numbers are set in Futura Condensed Bold. The body text is Palatino with Futura Heavy subheads. Tables and sidebars are set in Futura. The title of the book (on the cover and title pages) is set in Michelangelo.

RIDE THE WINDOWS™ WAVE

WITH BOOKS FROM VENTANA PRESS

Voodoo Windows, Second Edition

$24.95
282 pages, illustrated
ISBN:1-56604-145-7
Work Windows wizardry with productivity-enhancing tips. Organized by subject, this book offers a wealth of Windows techniques, shortcuts and never-before-published tricks that will streamline your daily tasks and save time. A great reference for beginners and experienced users alike.

The Official America Online for Windows Membership Kit & Tour Guide, Second Edition

$27.95
400 pages, illustrated
ISBN: 1-56604-128-7
America Online is the fastest-growing of all the commercial online services, and Ventana's outstanding guidebook is the official guide to this service. Download thousands of shareware files, take advantage of dozens of online publications (such as *USA Today, Time* and *National Geographic*), get stock quotes, join in forums with everyone from computer experts to famous musicians, and much, much more!

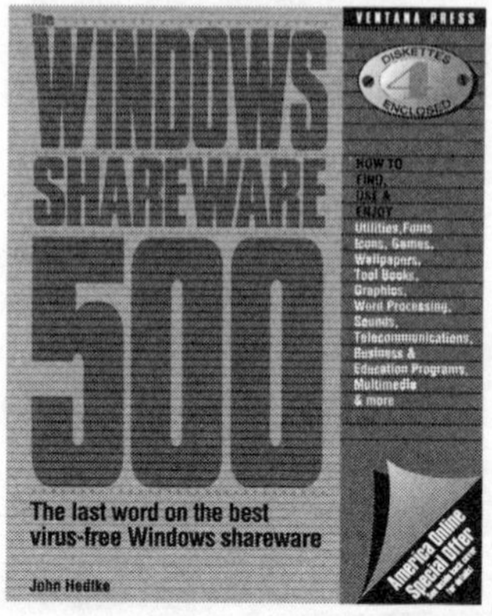

The Windows Shareware 500

$39.95
417 pages, illustrated
ISBN: 1-56604-045-0
The best Windows shareware available, from thousands of contenders. Includes utilities, sounds, fonts, icons, games, clip art, multimedia and more. BONUS: Four companion disks featuring top-rated programs, and an America Online membership disk along with 10 hours free online time!

The Windows Internet Tour Guide

$24.95
350 pages, illustrated
ISBN: 1-56604-081-7
Down with dreary UNIX commands! Trash the tedious text-based interface! At last, you can explore the infinite reaches of the Internet the right way: by pointing, clicking, dragging and dropping. *The Windows Internet Tour Guide* comes with everything you'll need to navigate the Internet with mouse-driven ease. Get the inside scoop on the Internet's offerings—how to get connected, tips on finding your way around, how to use the basic tools of the Net. Peruse a road map to the Internet's vast information resources. And use the enclosed software tools to convert the Internet's boring UNIX features to a face anyone will love!

Word for Windows Design Companion, Second Edition

$21.95
504 pages, illustrated
ISBN: 1-56604-075-2
Harness the design power of Word 6 with the help of hundreds of detailed, illustrated, annotated examples. Includes expert design advice and tips on all of Word's newest features and capabilities. Provides a springboard from word processing to help users at all levels get the most from their Word investment.

Desktop Publishing With Word for Windows, Second Edition

$21.95
352 pages, illustrated
ISBN: 1-56604-074-4
Gain design know-how and create attractive, persuasive documents in Word! Learn the basics of good design with step-by-step instructions from one of the world's foremost desktop designers. Includes an overview of Word 6 and detailed chapters on fonts, body and display type, graphics, style sheets and more.

ORDER TOLL-FREE

1-800-743-5369

	Quantity		Price		Total
Voodoo Windows	______	x	$19.95	=	$ ______
The Official America Online for Windows Membership Kit & Tour Guide, 2nd Edition	______	x	$27.95	=	$ ______
The Windows Shareware 500	______	x	$39.95	=	$ ______
The Windows Internet Tour Guide	______	x	$24.95	=	$ ______
Word for Windows Design Companion, 2nd Edition	______	x	$21.95	=	$ ______
Desktop Publishing With Word for Windows, 2nd Edition	______	x	$21.95	=	$ ______
Advertising From the Desktop	______	x	$24.95	=	$ ______
The Presentation Design Book, 2nd Edition	______	x	$24.95	=	$ ______
The Gray Book, 2nd Edition	______	x	$24.95	=	$ ______
Looking Good in Print, 3rd Edition	______	x	$24.95	=	$ ______
Newsletters From the Desktop, 2nd Edition	______	x	$24.95	=	$ ______
			Subtotal	=	$ ______

To order any Ventana Press title, fill out this order form and mail it to us with payment for quick shipment.

SHIPPING:

For all regular orders, please add $4.50/first book, $1.35/each additional.	=	$ ______
For "two-day air" on books, add $8.25/first book, $2.25/each additional.	=	$ ______
For orders to Canada, add $6.50/book.	=	$ ______
For orders sent C.O.D., add $4.50 to your shipping rate.	=	$ ______
North Carolina residents must add 6% sales tax.	=	$ ______
TOTAL	=	$ ______

CAN'T WAIT?

CALL OR FAX TOLL-FREE

☎ 800/743-5369

FAX 800/877-7955

(U.S. only)

Name ______________________ Company ______________________

Address (No PO Box) ______________________

City ______________________ State __________ Zip __________

Daytime Telephone ______________________

___ Payment enclosed ___VISA ___MC Acc't # ______________________

Expiration Date ______________ Interbank # ______________

Signature ______________________

Mail or fax to: Ventana Press, PO Box 2468, Chapel Hill, NC 27515 ☎ 919/942-0220 Fax 919/942-1140